Michael J. Weber

Invasion *of*

p r i v a c y

BIG Brother *and the* Company **Hackers**

Michael J. Weber

Invasion *of*

p r i v a c y

BIG Brother **and the** Company **Hackers**

Premier

General acknowledgment is made to the following for quoted material:

"Hairstyles and Attitudes" from Greetings from Timbuk 3—IRS. Copyright 1984 by Pat MacDonald.

"I'd Like to Teach the World to Sing": Artists: The New Seekers 1971-72; Words and Music by Roquel Davis, Roger John, Reginald Greenaway, Roger F. Cook, and William M. Backer.

All other trademarks are the property of their respective owners.

Important: Premier Press cannot provide software support. Please contact the appropriate software manufacturer's technical support line or Web site for assistance.

Premier Press and the author have attempted throughout this book to distinguish proprietary trademarks from descriptive terms by following the capitalization style used by the manufacturer.

Information contained in this book has been obtained by Premier Press from sources believed to be reliable. However, because of the possibility of human or mechanical error by our sources, Premier Press, or others, the Publisher does not guarantee the accuracy, adequacy, or completeness of any information and is not responsible for any errors or omissions or the results obtained from use of such information. Readers should be particularly aware of the fact that the Internet is an ever-changing entity. Some facts may have changed since this book went to press.

ISBN: 1-59200-043-6

Library of Congress Catalog Card Number: 2003101214

Printed in the United States of America

04 05 06 07 08 BH 10 9 8 7 6 5 4 3 2 1

Premier Press, a division of Course Technology
25 Thomson Place
Boston, MA 02210

SVP, Retail Strategic Market Group:
Andy Shafran

Publisher:
Stacy L. Hiquet

Senior Marketing Manager:
Sarah O'Donnell

Marketing Manager:
Heather Hurley

Manager of Editorial Services:
Heather Talbot

Associate Marketing Manager:
Kristin Eisenzopf

Project Editor:
Sandy Doell

Technical Reviewers:
Mirko Zorz and Berislav Kucan

Retail Market Coordinator:
Sarah Dubois

Copy Editor:
Cathleen Snyder

Interior Layout:
William Hartman

Cover Designer:
Mike Tanamachi

Indexer:
Kelly Talbot

Proofreader:
Kim Benbow

Dedicated to Dwain, Steve Kirsch, Jason Eric Smith, and countless others like them, who used technology to turn the tables on the technology that victimized them.

Acknowledgments

This book is a collaborative effort. I want to thank Stacy Hiquet (publisher), Sandy Doell (editor), Berislav Kucan and Mirko Zorz (tech editors), and Cathleen Snyder (copy editor) for their assistance and support.

Special thanks to George Kurtz, Steve Kirsch, Jason Eric Smith, Steve Gibson, A. Michael Froomkin, Ron Kessler, Sean "Jinx" Gailey, Epiphany, and Jeff Moss, for their cooperation and contributions.

About the Author

Michael J. Weber's career began on Madison Avenue where he produced hundreds of TV commercials, including several award winners, for top sponsors and ad agencies. He eventually landed in Hollywood and started writing screenplays. Weber has since written over a dozen scripts and episodic series for major film studios.

Invasion of Privacy is the second book written by Michael J. Weber in three years. His first, *Confessions of an Internet Auction Junkie,* was published by Prima in October 2000.

Dr. Timothy Leary introduced Weber to computing in 1979. A couple of years later he began budgeting TV commercials on the first IBM PC and an Apple 2. Weber has been a computer fanatic ever since!

Weber enjoys fun in the sun and lives in Los Angeles, California, and Palm Beach, Florida, with his Lhasa Apso Buddy.

Contents at a Glance

Part II
Zone Defense

Contents

Chapter 7
The Cheap Toothpick Syndrome 93

Chapter 8
The Metaphysics of Hacking 99

Chapter 9
Media Meltdown 131

Chapter 10
Badvertising 157

Introduction

thought I knew something about technology when I started writing this. Perhaps I did, but over the course of my research the world changed, I changed, and technology changed perhaps more than anything else. One dollar invested in the NASDAQ when my research began was worth about 19 cents by the time I got around to writing about the Internet boom (and bust). When I began this investigation the greatest threat to technology was the Y2K bug. Now it's cyber-terrorism!

The list is a long one. Denial-of-service attacks (DDoS) and killer Internet worms like Nimda, Code Red, and MSBlast were virtually unheard of when I began my research. I'm not one hundred percent certain, but to the best of my knowledge the phrase "identity theft" did not yet exist.

While I researched this book, the tech boom fizzled, the Internet bubble burst, the NASDAQ collapsed, and Al Qaeda attacked America on September 11, 2001. In essence, this book is about the technological and legal ramifications of all that. What I fear most from the fallout has been dubbed "the death of privacy" by noted law professor and cyber-privacy expert A. Michael Froomkin. The institutions and corporations we trust most have begun hacking us, suggests Froomkin in his article entitled "The Death of Privacy?" published in *the Stanford Law Review.*

Big business and Big Brother are the biggest hackers of all! Technology has become a nasty business. You know what I'm talking about: pop-up ads, cookies, spyware, spam, junk faxes, junk mail, telemarketing calls. You're a target and your personal information is a commodity! It is systematically harvested by information brokers with vast databases that do nothing but spit out computer profiles 24 hours a day. A nice fat dossier all about you is available for under a hundred bucks at your friendly neighborhood information broker! Unfortunately, most people don't realize that.

Technology, advertising, the media, and government have converged to invade our privacy. This book exposes the dangers (Part I) and proposes a practical defense (Part II).

What You'll Find in This Book

Invasion of Privacy is about people; people who do good and evil things with technology, people who are victims of technology, and victims who become avengers by turning the tables on the technology that victimizes them. The trouble with most technology books is that they read like they were written by a computer. A computer could not have written *Invasion of Privacy* because it consists of stories about people!

You'll meet Steve Kirsch, a Silicon Valley multimillionaire who sued the company that inundated him with junk faxes for $2.2 trillion dollars. You'll meet Jason Eric Smith, a struggling college student who set up a sting worthy of Paul Newman and Robert Redford when a con artist ripped-off his Apple PowerBook in an eBay auction. You'll meet Dwain and many hackers like him who anonymously save our butts!

I sought input from leading experts in the fields of computer security and privacy, such as George Kurtz, Steve Gibson, Ron Kessler, and Michael Froomkin, to provide you with practical steps you can take to protect your privacy, your personal information, and yourself. If you enjoy reading a good mystery, *Invasion of Privacy* is for you!

This Book Is for You If

> ➤ You hate being spied on.
> ➤ You hate spam, junk faxes, and telemarketing calls.
> ➤ You hate pop-up ads, cookies, spyware, and computer viruses.
> ➤ You hate to see TV commercials destroy old rock n' roll classics.
> ➤ You want to know if Mac is more secure than Windows.
> ➤ You're curious about what Microsoft is really up to.
> ➤ You want to know if the Internet bubble burst because of Napster.
> ➤ You wonder if Google could have prevented 9/11.
> ➤ You want to protect your privacy and personal information.

How This Book Is Organized

Part I, "The Invasion," exposes the forces (technology, advertising, the media, big business, and government) that have converged to invade our privacy. It illustrates the threat, profiles the players, and unmasks the spies in our midst.

Part II, "Zone Defense," presents a practical guide to protect your privacy, personal information, and self, in various zones where your privacy is subject to invasion; such as on your computer, surfing the Web, and while you're in public.

Keeping the Book's Content Current

Please visit the *Invasion of Privacy* website at http://www.mjweber.com/iop/privacy.htm for links, breaking news, software, research, and the latest information.

PART I
The Invasion

In a sense this is the next chapter of my last book, *Confessions of an Internet Auction Junkie*, which was published in October 2000. That's when my research began. This was supposed to be a follow-up called *Confessions of A Hacker*. It was a done deal, as they say in the book biz, until the publishing company changed hands and the deal fell through. The past is history, the future a mystery, and the present is a gift. That's why they call it "*the present.*" I view it this way. If I'd written that book then, I wouldn't have had the opportunity to write *Invasion of Privacy* now. Much has changed. One dollar invested in the NASDAQ when my research began on this book was worth approximately 19 cents by the time I wrote the first chapter.

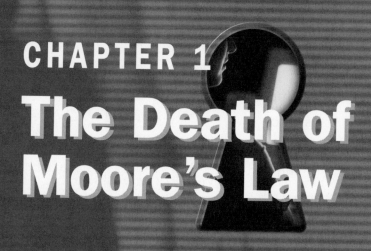

CHAPTER 1

The Death of Moore's Law

Koyaanisqatsi

- ➤ **The Tech Boom, Moore's Law, and the Next Killer App**
- ➤ **The Tech Slowdown**
- ➤ **Spy Technology**
- ➤ **The Dirty Little Secret**

I'm one of the geeks who lined up at Computer City at the stroke of midnight on August 15, 1995 to be the first kid on his block to install Windows 95. Technology turns me on! I began computing in 1981, budgeting films and commercials on the first IBM 8086. Later I worked on an Apple 2 and a Macintosh. I bought my first computer in 1987; an Epson Equity 286 with a 12-MHz CPU, 640 KB of RAM, and a whopping 40 MB hard drive. That killer machine set me back three grand with a VGA monitor and WordPerfect 3 installed, but it also set me free! It cost $1,000 to have a screenplay typed in Hollywood back then. Memorizing one WordPerfect macro on that Epson would change the entire course of my life. "Ctrl+Shift+F7+F7+F7," WordPerfect's renowned left/right margin reverse Tab indent × 3—which produces perfectly formatted character dialogue slots—empowered screenwriters like me to type their own screenplays and put a slew of good script typists out of work. That macro was the beginning of my love affair with technology!

Fifteen years later I can build a computer from scratch and tweak Windows so it hardly ever crashes, but I'm no hacker. I'm a writer who is curious about the impact of technology. That curiosity compelled me to investigate hacking. I started monitoring hacker Web sites like attrition.org, Cult of the Dead Cow, happyhacker.org, mobsters.net, hexzero.com/forum, and digicrime.com, as well as security sites like Helpnet Security.org and Foundstone. I reached out to experts like Jeff Moss, the founder of DEFCON and the Black Hat Briefings. At one point Jeff and I even explored collaborating on *Confessions of A Hacker* together. Neither the book nor the collaboration materialized, but as fate would have it, Mirko Zorz and Berislav Kucan, the founders of Helpnet Security are the technical editors of this book.

The further I delved into the subject of hacking and security, the more paranoid I became. I was getting the living heck, or to be precise, the "living hack," scared out of me! Not by hackers. Hackers go down in my book as heroes. I was scared by what hackers are fighting for: our freedom, security, and privacy! I was clueless. I had no idea of the threat the dark side of technology posed to our civil liberties. Did you ever head in a particular direction and wind up someplace else? That's what happened to me. I set out to write a book about hacking and ended up writing a book about the evils of technology!

The word *hacker* was originally coined to describe programmers who got their jollies by sharing their work with their colleagues, like Linus Torvalds did with open Linux code in 1991. Underlying a hacker's technical creations—such as the Internet and the personal computer—are the ethical values that produce them. This has been dubbed *The Hacker Ethic* by Torvalds, who is the coauthor of a book bearing this title. Technology remained relatively benign until the late 1990s, when the tech boom that fueled the decade fizzled out. That's when I began to notice that technology was becoming a malignant force!

The Tech Boom, Moore's Law, and the Next Killer App

On a bell curve, our privacy has declined at the same rate that the Central Processing Unit has advanced! I'm certain Gordon Moore, Intel's cofounder and Chairman Emeritus, didn't have that in mind in 1965 when he articulated "Moore's Law"—the hypothesis that *"transistor density on a manufactured die will double every year."* But there's a direct corollary! The threat to our privacy has increased in direct proportion to the power of the CPU. In fact, our personal information remained relatively secure until the mid-nineties, when the Pentium-class computer equipped with Windows 95 and a 28 kbps modem converged with the Internet.

Moore's Law was half of the equation that sparked the technology boom. The other component was the quest for "the next killer app." In the early days, the CPU was in a constant race to catch up with the latest software. I upgraded computers three times between 1987 and 1992, from a 286, to a 386, to a 486. This boded very well for Intel! Why upgrade so often? To keep pace with the next killer app. Computers were slower than molasses back then. In the history of personal computing, there has only been a handful of killer apps. By "killer app" I'm not simply referring to software applications, although software was the first killer app. I define "killer app" as any computer application or peripheral that sparks the need to upgrade to the next generation of computers! Today, iPods and digital cameras are the next killer app. Here are some others:

➤ The spreadsheet

➤ The word processor

➤ The database

➤ The Windows/Mac GUI interface

➤ Desktop publishing

➤ The Web browser

➤ The Internet

➤ E-mail

➤ Digital imaging

➤ MP3 (digital compression)

➤ CD-RW

➤ File sharing

➤ 3D gaming

➤ Broadband

➤ WI-FI

➤ Digital video editing

➤ Convergence

The personal computer was initially a dud. The public at large showed little interest or inclination in buying one until Lotus 1-2-3 and Corel WordPerfect hit the shelves and sparked the mass computer revolution. Do you know what differentiates the computer from every other machine on the planet? Every machine was invented to do something, except the computer! The computer was the first machine ever invented to do nothing. What is a computer without an operating system, besides an expensive doorstop? Software can do a variety of things; that's why programs are called applications. But what can a computer do without software? Nothing! What can a computer do with software? Virtually anything!

The Tech Slowdown

There will always be a next killer app, but Moore's Law is dead and gone. The beginning of the end came in 1997 with the birth of the Pentium II. Its introduction, which coincided with the launch of Windows 98 and a slew of new 32-bit apps optimized for Microsoft's latest and greatest operating system, marked a historic turning point. For the first time since the inception of the tech boom, software was playing catch-up with the CPU. The Pentium II was a fast chip! It had enough horsepower to drive any application, especially when equipped with 128 MB of RAM, a cutting-edge graphics co-processor, and a cavernous hard disk. The result was that people didn't need to upgrade their computers as often. I've owned six computers in my lifetime. I bought the first three in a five-year span. Had I continued at that rate, I'd be on my ninth computer today. But I only bought three computers over the next ten years. My consumption dropped fifty percent! This didn't bode well for Intel, or the tech boom.

I'm writing this book on a Dell laptop powered by a Pentium III 866 MHz CPU. I admit I'm no gamer, but by my standards it's still a pretty exotic machine. It has the best LCD screen-resolution money can buy—1600×1200. Practically every 18-inch flat panel on the market today has a maximum resolution of 1280×1024, not as crisp as my Dell! There are 1,486 MP3 files stored on one of its two 30-GB hard drives, all ripped from my personal CD collection, as well as thousands of gigantic image files. I can build and publish Web sites, design graphics, process images, write screenplays and books, watch DVDs, and burn my own CDs. Not bad for an eight-pound computer! Sometimes I daydream about buying a new cutting-edge Pentium 4 or Athlon 64, and no doubt I will. But I can afford to wait, and here's the reason. Do you want to know the difference in speed between my present computer and the fastest machine on the market? How fast can you blink?

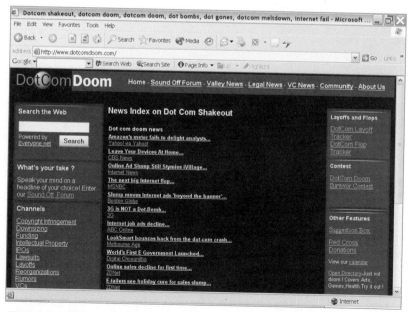

Figure 1.1 *Dot–com Doom*

The death of Moore's Law marked the end of the tech boom and the bull market that stampeded alongside. From Silicon Valley to Silicon Alley, dot-coms dropped like flies. Sites like BubbleEconomy.com, Dotcomfailures.com, Startupfailures.com, and Dotcom_Graveyard.com sprang up just to keep track of the body count. In 2001, the last year *Fortune Magazine* kept such a tally, it reported that 384 dot-com companies filed for bankruptcy. That doesn't sound like much on paper until you consider the shattered dreams and crushed lives each failure represents. Bow your head and take a moment to say dot-com Kaddish.

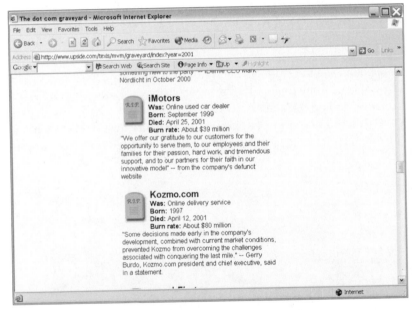

Figure 1.2 *In memoriam*

In Memoriam 2001—R.I.P.

A   Acusa.com, Adicom Wireless, Adornis.com, AdventureSeek.com, Air Media.com, Akamba, Allinstruments.com, Alltrue.com, Amesplace.com, Andy's Garage Sale, Art.com, Arzoo.com, AsSeenIn.com, Assetrack.com, Audiocafe.com, Audiohighway.com, AutoHoo.com, Automatic Media, Autovia.net, Avenew.com

B   Babygift.com, Balducci.com, Beenz.com, BEME.com, BePaid.com, Beseen, BestSelf, Bidland, BigEye.com, Bikeshop.com, Biztravel.com, BostonHockey.com, Box.com, BoysToys.com, BrowseSafe.com, B2Boxes.com, BuildNet, BuyItNow.com, ByeByeNOW.com

In Memoriam 2001—R.I.P. (continiued)

C CalendarCentral, CarClub.com, CashWars, CDworld.com, CertifiedTime.com, Chapbooks.com, Charitableway, Checkout.com, Chemdex, Chromatis Networks, Citiquest.com, CKGMedia.com, ClinicManager.com, Clip2, ClubComputer.com, ClubWallStreet.com, Collectibletown.com, CollegeHire.com, Colo.com, Comdisco.com, ComLinx, Communities.com, CompleteBackOffice.com, ConsumerCoupons.com, Contentville, Convey.com, Cottontails.com, CountryCool.com, Covad Communications, Creditunionmarketing.com, Crossrail.com, CyberCash, Cyber Cyclery, Cybergold, Cyberpix, CyberRebate.com

D Daily Radar, Dash.com, DayPlan.com, Dell Marketplace, Denmans.com, DESTIA.com, DietRehab.com, Digital Goods, DoDots, Done.com, Dreamticket.com, DriveOff.com, Dynaptics

E eAlity, Eazel, eCampus.com, eCircles.com, eContributor.com, eCountries, eCoverage, Egarden.com, Egghead.com, eHow, eMadison, eMarker.com, eMarketWorld.com, Ememories.com, Employeeservice.com, ePod, Eppraisals.com, Equidity, eRegister, Ereo, eSave.com, Essential.com, eTantrum, Etera, Etown.com, eToys, EverythingEducational.com, ExchangePath, Excite@Home,.Exodus Communications, Express.com, eYada.com, Ez2get

F FarmandCountry.com, FedCenter.com, FilmAxis.com, Financialprinter.com, FiredUp.com, Firetalk, FirstAuction.com, FitForAll.com, Flooz.com, Flowers2u.com, Flywheel Communications, Foodscape.com, FoodUSA.com, For.Net Technologies, 4MyCommunity.com, FreeEdu.com, FreeRealTime.com, Freeworks, Fullconcept.com, Funbug.com, FurnitureAndBedding.com

G GatherRound.com, Gavelnet.com, GeneralSearch.com, Globalaxxess.com, GlobalSpeedway.com, GlobexPharma.com, Gocowboy.com, GoNorCal.com, GOprinter, goRefer.com, GoShip.com, GoToWorld.com, Gotsavings.com, govWorks, Grantseeker.com, GreatEntertaining.com, Greenhouse for Startups

H Handtech, Handyman Online, Harbor-Net.com, HardwareStreet.com, Haseverything.com, HauteDecor, HealthCentral.com, HealthOnLine.com, Healthquick.com, HealthyCorp.com, HearMe, Homebytes.com, HomeRuns.com, Homes.com, HomeSmart.com, Hookt.com, HorizonScripts.com, HotOffTheWire.com, Hotpalm.com, Hotyellow98.com, Hyperdrive.com

I IAM.com, iCOMS, iDolls.com, iEmily.com, iExchange, Imamogram.com, iMotors.com, Impower, Improvementonline.com, Ingredients.com, InsideTheWeb, iPolitics.com, IPOptical, iProperty, iServed.com, IServe Internet, iTango, iTrackClaims.com, iTrainer.com, iTravel.com, Itribe.com, Ixpres.com

J Jobs.com, Jumpmusic.com, Justarrive, Just4Biz.com

In Memoriam 2001—R.I.P. (continiued)

K   Kerbango, KOZ.com, Kozmo

L   LAinsider.com, Lease-Etal.com, Lechters.com, Lendnetwork.com, Lipstream, Loansbid.com, LocalBusiness.com, Localmusic.com, Lucy.com

M   marchFirst, MaritimeDirect.com, Marketeye.com, Maverix.net, MaxRate.com, Mbrane, MDvista.com, Mediabrowser.com, Media3Net.com, Medque.com, Megacart.com, MerchantOnline, MetaMarkets.com, Micromatix.com, MilitaryHub.com, MortgageBid.com, MSHOW.com, Mustang.com, MyFreeLD.com, Mypsych.com, mySEASONS.com, Myspace.com, MyTurn.com

N   nCommand.com, Netfolio, NetMorf, NetSales, Next50.com, NorthPoint Communications, Npoint, NVST.com

O   OfficeClick.com, Office.com, Ohaha, Onfree.com, OnlineChoice, Ontheroad.com, OutdoorLiving, OutletZoo.com, Owners.com

P   PacketSwitch.com, PaperExchange.com, PaperX, Party411.com, PaxZone.com, PaydayTodayUSA.com, PCSales.com, PermitsNOW, Pharmasmarket.com, PhotoHighway.com, Physiciansite.com, PlanetRx.com, PogoPet.com, Policast.com, PortableLife.com, PrimeShot, Promptu, ProNetLink.com, ProofSpace, Publicaccesstechnology.com

Q   Qode.com, QueRico.com, Quokka Sports

R   Radnet, Realcomedy.com, Refer.com, Rel-Tyme.com, ReptileCenter.com, ResumeCard.com, reXnow.com, RNetHealth.com, RockCool.com, Rx.com

S   SafetyCop.com, Safety Director.com, SamtheRecordman.com, Sayshe.com, Sega.com, Send.com, ServiSense.com, Sevant.com, Shades.com, Shoppingtrend.com, SimpleSearch.com, SitesNet.com, Skyfish.com, SmithAgency.com, Snaz.com, Sneeker.com, Soapbox.com, Sparks.com, Special Car Journal.com, SportBrain, SportChip.com, Starbelly.com, Stario.com, Stocktalklive.com, StreamSearch.com, Streetsheets.com, StreetZebra.com, St3.com, Support123.com, Surfmiles.com, Swapit.com, Sx Sportsmed.com, Syscon USA.com

T   Taxes4Less.com, TechnologyConnect.com, Technology Today.com, TerraShare, The Digital Dog, The Learning Studio.com, TheCompost, TheCustomShop.com, Theglobe.com, THELIVINGLIBRARY.com, Themestream, TheStandard.com, TheTradesGuild.com, ThinkLink, Third Voice, 3merge.com, 3Re, 3ZNET.com, Ticketplanet.com, Timebuy.com, Top Tutors.com, Total E.com, ToysInternational.com, Travelago, TravelNavigator.com, Travel-Now.com

U   UltimateBid, Unexplored.com, USDataCenters, Utilimax.com, Utility.com, U-TOK.com

---

In Memoriam 2001—R.I.P. (continiued)

V   Valuewine.com, Valusport dot com, VCityNet.com, VetAlliance.com, Vitamins.com, Volume.com, Voter.com, VoyagerToys.com

W   Wall of Sound, WebRadio.com, WebRx.com, WebSwap, Webvan, Wine.com, WolfXpress.com, Work.com, Workz.com, Worldprints.com, WorldSpy.com, Wwwrrr

X   Xigo, XS-Media

Z   Z.com, Zideo.com, Zing.com, ZoneNetwork.com, Zoza.com, Zydeco.com

---

It's no coincidence that the dark side of technology emerged at the end of the tech boom. The Hopi Indians have a word, *koyaanisqatsi*, which means nature out of balance. That's what happened to technology. The hallmark of success had always been innovation. After the tech shakeout, the paradigm shifted. The new hallmark that defined success became technology that turned a profit. The gyp was on! Silicon Valley went to work inventing technology to nickel-and-dime the public. Click-tracks, Web bugs, spyware, pop-ups, spam servers, war-dialing, junk faxes, prerecorded telemarketing bots: technology that harvests personal information and invades our privacy became the next killer app!

Spy Technology

You're under surveillance. People are spying on you! You're being profiled and targeted. There's a big fat file on a supercomputer that contains everything there is to know about you, and that information is for sale! Here's what a hundred bucks can buy from an Internet information broker like USSEARCH.com. Put yourself in Jane's shoes.

Search Name: SUBJECT, JANE C

Search ID Number: 2524523

Most Recent Information

Name: Subject, Jane C
AKA:
Current Address: 1234 Main St Anywhere
L.A., CA 90061
Los Angeles County

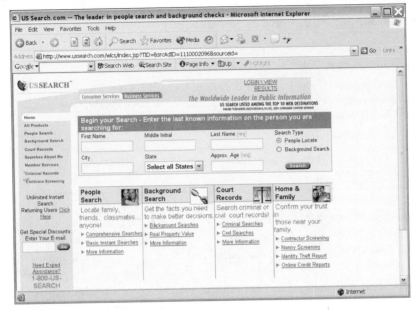

Figure 1.3 *USSEARCH.com site*

Listed Phone Numbers at 1234 Main St Anywhere, CA

555-555-6789

Property Ownership at 1234 Main St Anywhere, CA

Primary Owner: Subject, Jane
Site Address: 1234 Main St
Anywhere, CA 90061-1234
Owner Address: 1234 Main St
Anywhere, CA 90061-1234
Telephone: 555-555-6789
APN: 1111-0000-011
Assessed Value: $371,441.00

Individuals Reported at 1234 Main St Anywhere, CA

Subject, Mary
1234 Main St Anywhere, CA 90061

Subject, Steve
1234 Main St Anywhere, CA 90061
1111 Windy Way #1 Anywhere, CA 90001

Subject, Mary
1234 Main St Anywhere, CA 90061
7555 Westgate Ave Anywhere, CA 90144
12 E Bonnie Ave Anywhere, CA 90055

Subject, Maria
AKA: Subject, Ari
1000 Deerbox Ct Anywhere, CA 95242
1234 Main St Anywhere, CA 90061
2121 S Country Jam Blvd Anywhere, CA 95204

Subject, Cyndi
AKA: Subject, Cynthia
POB: 1111 Anywhere, VA 20188
2222 333rd Anywhere, VA 20188
9001 South Pl Anywhere, CA 90230
9003 South Pl Anywhere, CA 90230
1234 Main St Anywhere, CA 90061

Possible Neighbors of 1234 Main St Anywhere, CA

Neighbor, Steven
1233 Main St Anywhere, CA

Neighbor, Greg
1231 Main St
Anywhere, CA 90064 Los Angeles County

Neighbor, Jack
12353 Main St
Anywhere, CA 90064 Los Angeles County

Neighbor, Jane
1237 Main St
Anywhere, CA 90064 Los Angeles County

10-Year Address History Associated with Your Search

The addresses listed below may indicate a residence or other address used
by your subject or another person with the same name. Addresses are usually listed in order of currency.

1: 1234 Main St Anywhere, CA 90061
L.A., CA 99999
Listed Phone Numbers: 555-555-6789
Property Ownership: See above

2: 3456 Long St, Anywhere, CA 99999
Listed Phone Numbers at 3456 Long St, Anywhere, CA
No information on file

Property Ownership at 3456 Long St, Anywhere, CA

Primary Owner: Owner, George
Site Address: 3456 Long St
Anywhere, CA 90066-2009
Owner Address: 1111 Lake St
Anywhere, CA 90069-1003
Telephone: 310-555-5555
APN: 9876-0094-001
Account #:
Assessed Value: $50,473.00

Individuals Reported at 3456 Long St, Anywhere, CA

Subject, David
3456 Long St, Anywhere, CA 90066

Subject, Steve
1234 Main St Anywhere, CA 90061
1111 Windy Way #1 Anywhere, CA 90001

Subject, Mary, B
AKA: Subject, Marie
6789 Lowe Ave Anywhere, CA 90405
3456 Long St, Anywhere, CA
0501 Wilshire Blvd. #225 Anywhere, CA 90211

Subject, Robert
4242 Marina Dr #1 Anywhere, CA 90299
3456 Long St, Anywhere, CA
9876 Shel St Anywhere, CA 90210

Subject, John
3109 Lowe St Anywhere, CA 90405
2999 Gilbert Ave Anywhere, CA 90066

Possible Neighbors of 2999 Gilbert Av Anywhere, CA 90066

Neighbor, Bill
2998 Gilbert Ave
Anywhere, CA 90066 Los Angeles County

Neighbor, Peter
2997 Gilbert Ave
Anywhere, CA 90066 Los Angeles County

Neighbor, Michael
2996 Gilbert Ave
Anywhere, CA 90066 Los Angeles County

Neighbor, Tom
2995 Gilbert Ave
Anywhere, CA 90066 Los Angeles County

Neighbor, Guy
2994 Gilbert Ave
Anywhere, CA 90066 Los Angeles County

The Following Databases Were Searched but Yielded No Results

Bankruptcies, Tax Liens & Civil Judgments.....No records found

National Death Index.........................No records found

Drug Enforcement Agency......................No records found

FAA Airmen..................................No records found

FAA Aircraft................................No records found

National Coast Guard Merchant Vessels.........No records found

Marriage Index..............................No records found

Divorce Index...............................No records found

On Premise County Courthouse Search Results

Subject Name: Subject, Jane C
Jurisdiction: Los Angeles, CA
Yrs Searched—Higher Court: 7
Yrs Searched—Lower Court: 7
Yrs Searched—Extra:
Results:
Search Abstract
Case Number: 123456
Charge: 1 VC 23153(a) D.U.I. Causing Injury -(F)
Dispo: Dismissed
Charge: 2 VC 23153(b) D.U.I. Causing Injury with BAC=>.08% -(F)
Dispo: Pleaded no contest…Charge 2
Sentence: 2 years state prison; 3 years formal probation.

Offense Date:
Arrest Date:
File Date: 6/30/94
Dispo Date: 8/26/94
Gen Disp.:
ID Note:
Special Notes (if any): No other convictions found

Civil Lawsuit Search Results

(State and county of last reported address searched)
Subject: Subject, Jane C
Search: County Civil-7 Yr
Area: Miami-Dade
Search Date: 05/31/1993–05/31/2000
Court: Dade Circuit Court
State: FL
County: Dade
Type: Upper
Plaintiff: Jane C Subject
Defendant: John Smith (MD)
Case Number: 12-12345-AA-08
Amount: $3000.00
File Date: 12/13/96
Status Date: 05/21/98
Status Type: Order of dismissal
Verified By: Name only
Comments: COA: Professional malpractice
Search Date: 05/31/1993–05/31/2000
Court: Dade Circuit Court
State: FL
County: Dade
Type: Upper
Plaintiff: Acme Mortgage Lending Inc.
Defendant: Jane C Subject
Case Number: 12-12345-AA-09
Amount: N/A
File Date: 07/12/96
Status Date: 08/26/97
Status Type: Dismissed
Verified By: Name only
Comments: COA: Mortgage foreclosure

The Dirty Little Secret

Here's technology's dirty little secret. Do you know who's spying on you? The institutions you trust most! Banks, insurance carriers, credit cards, public records, phone, cable, ISPs, advertisers, media, software developers, retailers, supermarkets, and Internet portals sit up nights dreaming of ways to profit from the confidential information we provide. They trick us into trusting them—into ratting ourselves out—and then they sell our secrets to the highest bidder!

Unfortunately, once personal information is in the public domain, it's out there in perpetuity. You can't put the toothpaste back in the tube, but you can screw the cap back on! This book explains how. Think of it as an elaborate video game. You're the target! People are spying on you. Technology is a double-edged sword, their weapon and your shield. This book is your scorecard. It will reveal who the players are, the means by which they spy on us, and appropriate countermeasures to foil them. The ultimate defense is stealth! Spies can't spy on what they can't see. This book will teach you how to construct a virtual firewall between the spies and your life!

CHAPTER 2
The Target Is You!

Layers, Players, and Privacy Zones

"Hairstyles and attitudes, how are they connected? Are the styles we embrace a matter of taste or values rejected? Hairstyles and attitude, how do they relate? How well do we use our freedom to choose the illusions we create?"

—Timbuk 3

Did you ever see one of those movies where the bad guys plant a bug on the hero without his knowledge and then track him everywhere he goes? That's what happened to you! As you can see in the figure, you are a bull's-eye surrounded by various layers: business, media, advertising, technology, and government. On each layer there is an assortment of *players* who each want a piece of your hide! To accomplish this they employ technology to spy on you. If a picture is worth a thousand words, the illustration tells the story of this book.

Figure 2.1 *The Target illustration*

The Player Table

A Who's-Who on who is spying on you:

The Players

Business	Wall Street, Retailers, Banks, Credit cards, Insurance, Utilities, Supermarkets
Media	Hollywood, News, Television, Music, Publishing, Internet, Cable
Advertising	Madison Avenue, Information brokers, Sponsors, Double-click, Telemarketers, Junk faxes, Spammer
Technology	Hackers, Crackers, Identity thieves, Cyber-scammers, Security experts, Programmers, Microsoft, America Online
Government	Politicians, Lobbyists, The IRS, Police/FBI/military, Cyber-terrorists, Terrorists, Carnivore

Most of the players are in bed with each other, as you can see, just as the layers themselves are intertwined. The fingerprints of Wall Street, Madison Avenue, and Microsoft, for example, are virtually everywhere. Besides institutional players, your friends, neighbors, employers, and enemies may be spying on you as well! Why? Because information is power, and these players want control. They view you as a demographic, and they want your money, loyalty, and time.

Privacy Zones

As you can see in the next figure, you're surrounded by zones of privacy: The Public Zone, The Home Zone, The Computer Zone, and The Internet Zone, separated by a Technology Zone. No matter which zone you're in, you're susceptible to technology that has the potential to invade your privacy. The corresponding technologies are listed in the tables that follow.

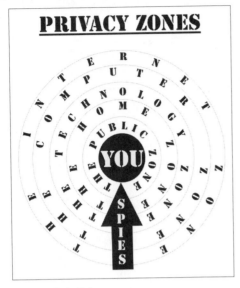

Figure 2.2 *Privacy zones*

The Public Zone

Digital Surveillance	Beeper tracking, Biometric recognition, ATMs
Aerial Surveillance	Photo enforcement, GPS tracking (On-Star), Speedpass
Cellular Surveillance	Closed-circuit video, Credit trail, Carnivore, RFID chips

The public space is a database.

The Home Zone

Telephone	Cell phone	Fax
Television	Cable TV	Satellite TV
Utilities		
WI-FI		

You're not alone when you're at home.

The Computer Zone

Hard Drive	Floppy Drive	Removable
File sharing	Viruses	Piracy
Operating system	Software	Drivers
Bugs and patches	Service packs	

Who knows what actually lurks on your computer?

The Internet Zone

ISP	Web Browser	Privacy/Security Settings
Cookies and Web bugs	Downloads	Shareware
Spyware	Worms	Spam
E-mail	Trojan horses	E-commerce
Instant messaging	File sharing	Web site privacy policies
Digital authentication	Google	Information brokers
Hackers	Crackers	pop-up ads

There is no privacy on the Internet.

Zone Defense

It's no coincidence that the most popular personal firewall on the Internet is called ZoneAlarm. Whatever zone you're in, you're susceptible to technology that can invade your privacy, but in most instances there are technological or physical countermeasures to prevent it. This book is a repository of counter-measures to help you build a "defensive zone" all around you! You'll need to tweak some security settings and install some software, but you don't have to be a computer whiz to do this. My last book, which dealt with Internet auctions, HTML, and e-commerce, was far more technical. The real objective of this book is to convince you to change your mindset because if you don't, you're a sitting duck!

You'll find links to download ZoneAlarm and other useful security utilities on the *Invasion of Privacy* homepage at http://www.mjweber.com/iop/privacy.htm.

Figure 2.3 *VeriSign trust logos × 3*

Trust

If you're old enough to read this book, you grew up in an era when it was safe to trust other people, institutions, and yourself. But nowadays trust is mar-keted like a candy bar. VeriSign sells its much-vaunted trust seal of approval for cold hard cash. Does that mean you should automatically trust every site that displays a VeriSign seal? Of course not! What's to stop an enterprising scam artist, for example, from downloading VeriSign's seals, just as I did for this book, and displaying them on his fly-by-night Web site? You've got to start using your head by connecting all the dots. Nowadays it's unwise to trust anyone, especially yourself. The first security leak you must plug is you.

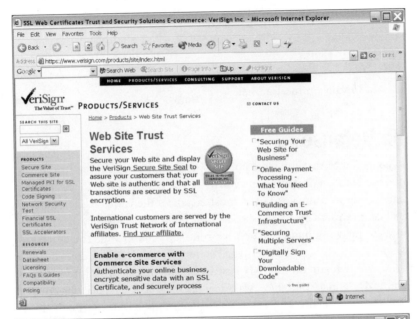

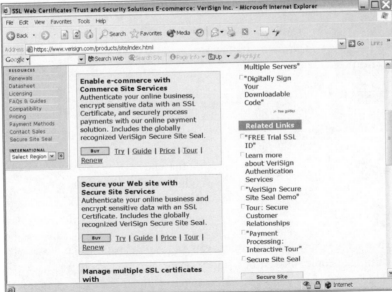

Figure 2.4 *VeriSign Web site*

We are programmed to trust other people. It's hardwired in our DNA. Think of yourself as a Manchurian candidate and of this book as your deprogramming tool. Programming—and trust, for that matter—is a product of habit. Protecting your privacy is as straightforward as changing some bad habits. But old habits die hard!

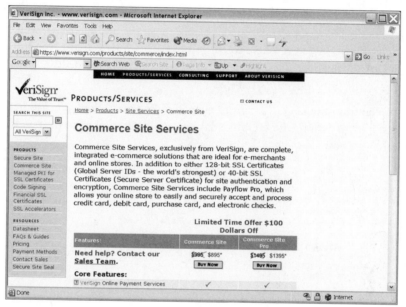

Figure 2.5 *VeriSign trust-for-sale page*

Rats and Habits

Take a lab rat. Place him in a maze with five tunnels and hide a piece of cheese at the end of one. What happens? The rat explores each tunnel until he finds the cheese. Now repeat the same experiment several times. What happens? The rat learns to skip the empty tunnels and heads straight for the cheese. Now alter the experiment. Move the cheese to a different tunnel. Does the rat give a rat's tail? No! He sniffs his way up each tunnel once again until he finds the cheese. To the rat it's just a big game. He plays because he loves cheese. Do you know the difference between human beings and lab rats? Lab rats have more common sense! In the game of life, the cheese gets moved (the rules get changed) all the time, but human beings paradoxically don't catch on when the cheese is gone. We blindly go down the same tunnel over and over again out of habit.

Habits are like the River of Life, longer than the great Mississippi and more powerful than the mighty Colorado. It was here long before you were and will be here long after you're gone. Each day you wake up and go through the daily ritual of preparing for your ride on the River of Life by habit! You brush your teeth, put on your clothes, sip some coffee, and then head down to the riverbank and put your rickety old canoe in the water. You have two choices: ride with the tide or paddle against it. Rowing against the River of Life is a backbreaking job! You must maintain balance, position, and direction, while paddling frantically to get where you're going. Each stroke you lose, you lose ground. And the river doesn't care what direction you're headed; it keeps flowing in the same direction it always has.

Take a cue from the lab rat. Learn to change old habits! Drop your paddle, sit back, and go with the flow. Or one day you could get trapped in the rapids without a life vest.

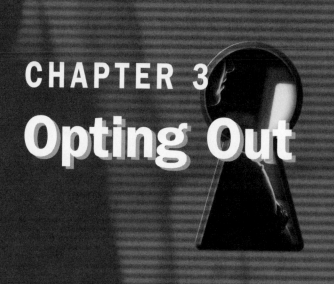

CHAPTER 3
Opting Out

Practicing Stealth: How to Create a Digital Doppelganger

➢ **The Digital Doppelganger: Garbage In, Garbage Out**

"Age is a number and mine is unlisted!"

—My mother

My mother, who has never touched a computer, has been practicing stealth her entire life. She grew up in an era when it was impolite to ask a lady's age and Jack Benny remained forever 39. Her friends might have found it a bit peculiar that my brother and I grew progressively younger as time marched on, but the ammunition to calculate her age has never crossed her lips! She wasn't fibbing, either. My mother was simply practicing stealth. The amazing thing is she beat the system, for a while at least!

Yahoo features a free People Search engine sponsored by USSEARCH.com, the same information broker that provided the report on Jane C. Subject in Chapter 1. Simply type in a last name, first name or initial, city, and state, and then click Search.

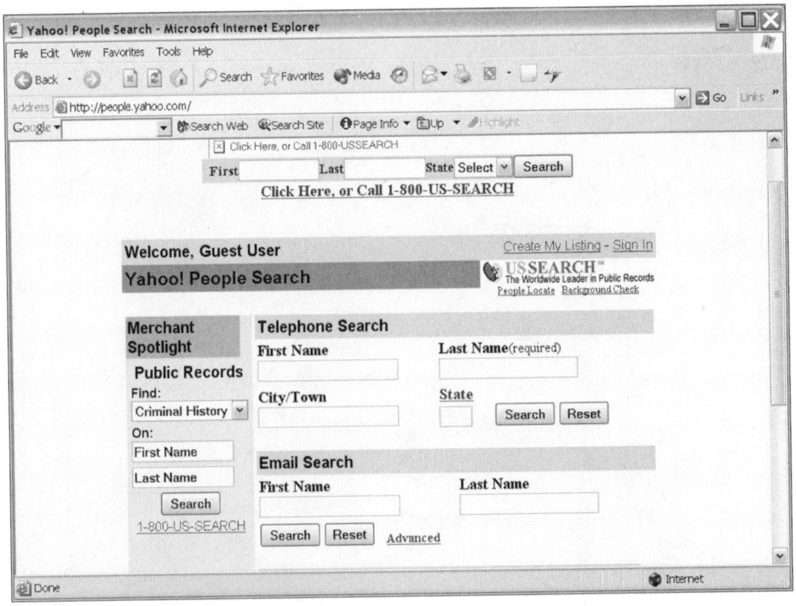

Figure 3.1 *Yahoo! People search page*

If you score an initial hit on the given name, you get an option to search the public records. A search box appears with the subject's name, and you're required to enter the person's state and approximate age. You click and voilà! A page appears with the exact age of almost every subject with that name.

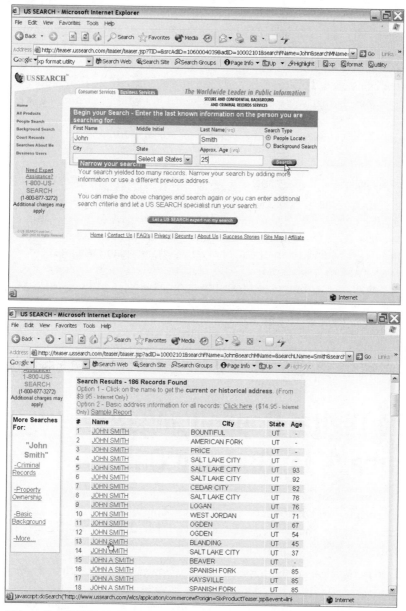

Figure 3.2 *USSEARCH.com public records search*

As you can see, some search records draw a blank when it comes to the subject's age. Not knowing my mother's actual age, I couldn't resist doing some research. I typed in her name, and the public records returned zilch! When I informed my mother she was among the handful who beat the system, she was absolutely delighted! Then she got a mischievous twinkle in her eyes and asked me to do an age search on some of her friends. I never did get around to it. Alas, that's not the end of the story. Not long ago, I was tracking down some lost friends on Yahoo! People Search for a birthday party. My mother recently purchased property in a different state, and I decided on a lark to do another age search. This time, her age registered! The moral of the story—if there is one—is that you can beat the system for a while, but nothing lasts forever! My mother has the right idea, though. She knows the system can be spoofed. That's the idea behind creating a *digital doppelganger*.

The Mythological Doppelganger

A doppelganger is a shadow-self that accompanies every human. Only the owner of a doppelganger can see it; otherwise, it is invisible to human eyes. Dogs and cats have been known to see doppelgangers. Providing sympathetic company, a doppelganger almost always stands behind a person, and casts no reflection in a mirror. Doppelgangers are prepared to listen and give advice to humans, either by implanting ideas in their heads or by a sort of osmosis. A doppelganger is said to be bad luck if it is seen, and rarely will it make itself visible to friends or family, which often causes great confusion. Doppelgangers can be mischievous and malicious.

The Digital Doppelganger: Garbage In, Garbage Out

The German etymology of the word "doppelganger" is "double-goer," a double, often ghostly, counterpart to self. The Monster was Victor's doppelganger in Mary Shelley's *Frankenstein*, and Mr. Hyde was Dr. Jekyll's doppelganger in Robert Louis Stevenson's classic novel.

A digital doppelganger is the technological equivalent of its mythological counterpart, a parallel self designed to protect your identity from the players who are invading your privacy. There's an old computer axiom: "garbage in, garbage out." A digital doppelganger fools the system into thinking you're somebody else, even if that somebody turns out to be nobody! Let's examine Superman's doppelganger.

Superman's Doppelganger
First name: Clark
Last name: Kent
Address: 1 Daily Planet Square
City: Metropolis
State: Illinois
Zip: 62960
Phone: 628-555-5518
Fax: 628-555-5519
E-mail: ckent@dailyplanet.com
Assistant: Jimmy Olsen
Supervisor: Perry White
Spouse: Lois Lane
Pet's Name: Krypto
Birth Date: 7-4-38
Mother's maiden name: Eben

The Golden Rule of Personal Information

When it comes to providing personal information, such as your name, address, phone number, fax number, e-mail address, employer, date of birth, mother's maiden name, or Social Security number, the Golden Rule is very simple:

When in doubt, leave it out!

You can fill in the blanks with anything you choose, as long as it isn't the truth! Isn't giving out bogus information being deceitful? Yes, but no more so than the institutions that exploit us and traffic in our personal information! Virtually every company we come in contact with employs technology to invade our privacy. Numerous variations are cited throughout this book. Your digital doppelganger will help level the playing field. But before you start using it, you've got to learn when it's applicable.

The Three-Ring Information Circus

There are three information rings—legal, contractual, and the "circus." You can only use a digital doppelganger in the circus ring. Following are the boundaries and rules pertaining to the provision of personal information in each ring.

The Legal Ring

You are legally bound to provide factual information to the following entities:

➤ Uncle Sam

➤ Law enforcement

➤ IRS

➤ DMV

➤ Your employer

➤ Your bank

➤ Your credit card company

➤ Your investment companies

➤ Your landlord

➤ Your insurance company

➤ Attorneys

The Contractor Ring

Provide information to contractors on a "need-to-know" basis. It's advantageous to restrict the factual information you provide in accordance with the pertinence of the service. You aren't obliged to tell the gas company your mother's maiden name, your date of birth, your Social Security number, your fax number, or your e-mail address, for example. They simply need to know your first name or initial, your last name, and your address. Entities in the contractor ring include

➤ Phone company

➤ Cell phone service provider

➤ Utilities

➤ Cable company

➤ ISPs

➤ Anything you subscribe to

There are two reasons to restrict the confidential information you provide to contractors.

1. They sell the information you provide and share it with others.
2. You are the sum of your digital breadcrumbs.

The Circus Ring

This circus ring is the domain of the digital doppelganger. Provide factual information at you own risk. No one in this information ring can be trusted!

➤ Web sites

➤ Retailers

➤ Supermarkets

➤ Health clubs

➤ Salespeople

➤ Telemarketers

➤ Market researchers

➤ Nosey neighbors

Before proceeding, grab a pencil and fill in the "My Digital Doppelganger" form. Remember, no factual information. The purpose of this exercise is to be a chameleon!

My Digital Doppelganger

First name: _____

Last name: _____

Address: _____

City: _____

State:_____ Zip: _____

Phone:_____ Fax:_____

E-mail: _____

Employer: _____

Supervisor: _____

Assistant: _____

Spouse's name: _____

Children's names: _____

Pet's name:_____

Mother's maiden name:_____

Date of birth:_____

Social Security number: _____

Congratulations! As soon as you begin using your digital doppelganger in the real world you'll notice a decline in spam, junk mail, telemarketing calls, and junk faxes. But it only works in the circus ring. So how do you protect your confidential information in the legal and contractor rings? In addition to the Golden Rule of personal information—When in doubt, leave it out—there's another option at your disposal. You can opt out of all your privacy agreements.

Opting Out

Without going into all the legal mumbo jumbo, a *privacy agreement* is a contract to "traffic in" and sell the personal information that you provide to various contractors. Opting out of a privacy agreement is your only means to keep the companies you deal with honest! The opt-out notice shown below accompanied a bill I recently received from Sprint. I immediately picked up the phone, dialed the toll-free number provided, and opted out of the agreement. It took less than a minute because I did it then and there. If you don't opt out of a privacy agreement contemporaneously, it ain't easy! What is the consequence of not opting out? If I hadn't, telemarketers would have my implicit permission to call me on my cell phone—on my dime—to peddle junk I don't give a hoot about.

Figure 3.3 *Sprint opt-out agreement cover*

Figure 3.4 *Sprint opt-out agreement inside*

Privacy Agreements

Let's examine a privacy agreement up close and personal. Amazon.com has a privacy agreement that you can access by clicking the Updated Privacy Notice link at the bottom of most of the site's pages. This is typical of most privacy agreements. The fine print makes your eyes glaze over, but in the parlance of the information business, "share" is the operative buzzword. Amazon's agreement states

Does Amazon.com "share" the information it receives?

Information about our customers is an important part of our business, and we are not in the business of selling it to others. We share customer information only as described below and with subsidiaries of Amazon.com, Inc.

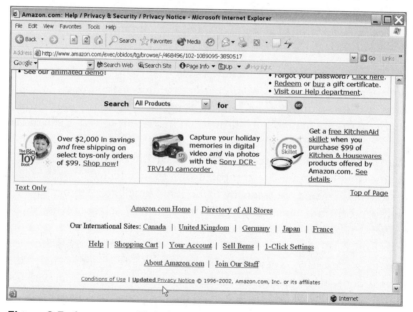

Figure 3.5 *Amazon.com Updated Privacy Notice link*

That sounds pretty reassuring until you read a bit further, do some clicking, and find out who Amazon's so-called "subsidiaries" are.

Affiliated Businesses We Do Not Control: We work closely with our affiliated businesses such as Marketplace, zShops, and Auctions sellers…. In other cases, we operate stores, provide services, or sell product lines jointly with businesses, [which include Toysrus.com,

Babiesrus.com, Imaginarium.com, Target, Circuit City, Borders, AT&T Wireless, Sprint, T-Mobile, CarsDirect.com, Hotwire, drugstore.com, The Vacation Store, Ofoto.com, Office Depot, J&R, and Virginmega.com].

Jeff Bezos always had the reputation of being a touchy-feely guy. As you can see, he's extremely trusting when it comes to sharing your information with other businesses that he admittedly doesn't control. Which begs the question, who do they share their information with? Amazon's list goes on:

> **Agents:** We employ other companies and individuals to perform functions on our behalf. Examples include fulfilling orders, delivering packages, sending postal mail and e-mail, removing repetitive information from customer lists, analyzing data, providing marketing assistance, processing credit card payments, and providing customer service. They have access to personal information needed to perform their functions, but may not use it for other purposes.

Amazon's list of "agents" could include virtually anybody, and Mr. Bezos is certainly more trusting than I would be that the information won't be used for extracurricular purposes. The Internet is replete with horror stories that highlight the misuse of personal information. In a recent speech, Richard H. Brown, the chief executive of technology giant EDS, stated, "The danger to the digital economy's longevity is not from the bursting of the dot-com bubble. Those effects are minuscule compared with those inflicted by breaches of trust." He cited Toysmart, a company that offered to sell its customer records (including credit card numbers and children's names) as part of its bankruptcy settlement as one glaring example of the digital economy's growing breach of trust. What guarantee does Amazon give that the personal information its agents have access to will not be used for another purpose? Absolutely none, unless you believe Amazon can protect your privacy with lip service! Amazon's list of information-sharing stipulations continues.

> **Business Transfers:** As we continue to develop our business, we might sell or buy stores, subsidiaries, or business units. In such transactions, customer information generally is one of the transferred business assets but remains subject to the promises made in any pre-existing Privacy Notice (unless, of course, the customer consents otherwise). Also, in the unlikely event that Amazon.com, Inc., or substantially all of its assets are acquired, customer information will of course be one of the transferred assets.

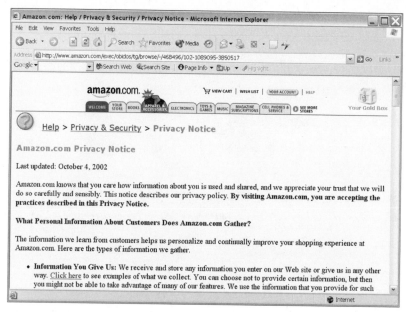

Figure 3.6 *Amazon.com privacy agreement*

Protection of Amazon.com and Others: We release account and other personal information when we believe release is appropriate to comply with the law; enforce or apply our Conditions of Use and other agreements; or protect the rights, property, or safety of Amazon.com, our users, or others. This includes exchanging information with other companies and organizations for fraud protection and credit risk reduction.

As you can see, not opting out of one privacy agreement makes your personal information available to dozens (if not hundreds) of third parties. And it's safe to assume these third parties share your information with other third parties, who in turn share it with other third parties. Do you see where this is going? Information is exponential! Before you know it, thousands of companies you've never heard of know all about you: your name, address, e-mail address, phone number, fax number, and cell number, employer, hobbies, buying patterns, the names of friends and family...and that's just the tip of the iceberg!

This final paragraph, buried in the middle of Amazon's privacy notice, provides the only sentence in the entire agreement that gives you an option to opt out. Do you see where it says, "please adjust your Customer Communication Preferences?"

Promotional Offers: Sometimes we send offers to selected groups of Amazon.com customers on behalf of other businesses. When we do this, we do not give that business your name and address. If you do not want to receive such offers, please adjust your Customer Communication Preferences.

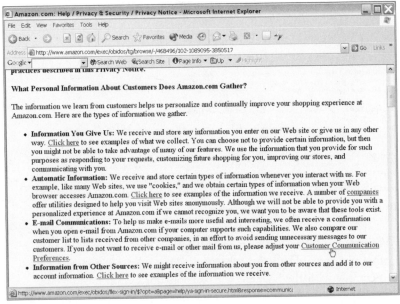

Figure 3.7 *Amazon.com Customer Communication Preferences link*

Click on Customer Communication Preferences, and you'll be directed to log on to your account. Enter your user name and password, and the opt-out page will appear. This is where you opt out from special offers, contests, promotions, research surveys, solicitations by Amazon.com's shopping partners, spam, junk mail, and all the petty annoyances and invasions of privacy that make you a sitting target. You'll note that everything is selected by default. Deselect everything that isn't essential. Here's a sample of my personal preferences. I deselected everything with the exception of

Send messages: *By e-mail only*

If you would like to receive e-mail messages: *Send text-only messages*

Display live order-status information while I shop: *Show me shipping and delivery estimates, important messages about my order*

Don't greet me by name when I visit other sites to make Honor System payments.

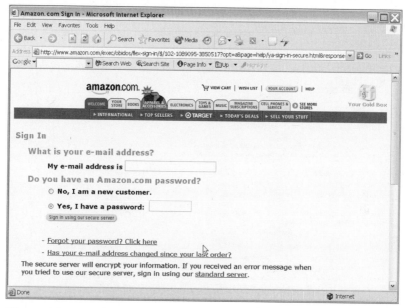

Figure 3.8 *Amazon.com customer logon page*

If you would prefer to receive only the most essential communication from us: *Send me only those messages related to my orders, listings, and bids.*

That's all there is to opting out!

The Golden Rule of privacy agreements is *always opt out*!

Where to Opt Out

You opt out of a privacy agreement the same place you opted in—by mail, phone, or on the Internet. The rule of thumb is unless you originally registered on the Internet, you'll most likely have to opt out by phone or mail. The best way to opt out is to respond immediately when you receive an opt-out notice, as I did with the Sprint notice that accompanied my monthly bill. Opt-out notices provide a toll-free number where you can use an automated system to opt out. Don't depend on a live operator to opt out for you. Request an opt-out number or Internet link from the operator, then opt out yourself.

Opting out on the Internet consists of following the drill I just outlined. Log on to every site with which you have an account, including ISPs, eBay, MSN, Yahoo, Amazon, AOL, DSL, digital cable, user groups, subscription sites, news services, chat, IM, game sites, and e-tailers, and locate their privacy agreements, which are usually at the bottom of the page. Now locate the link

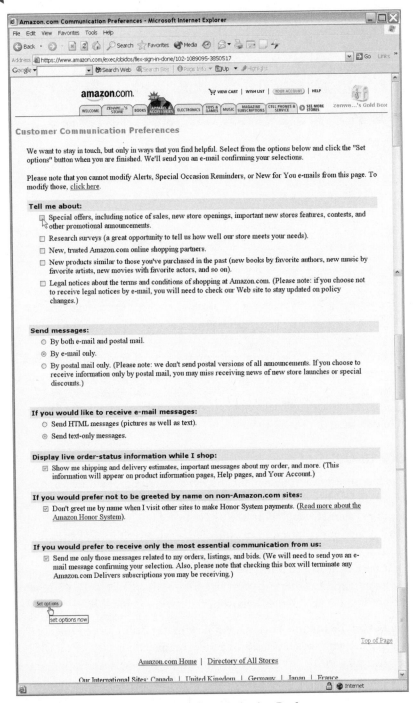

Figure 3.9 *Amazon.com Customer Communication Preferences page*

to the appropriate Customer Preferences page. Opting out isn't hard; it's merely repetitive and laborious! However, once you get the old stuff behind and begin to opt-out contemporaneously, it's no big chore.

Who to Opt Out From

Who do you have privacy agreements with? The same players surrounding you on the target illustration in the first figure in Chapter 2. Here's a hint: Who do you pay by check or credit card? From whom do you receive catalogs, magazines, spam, and junk mail? Phone, cell phone, cable TV, electric, gas, ISP, bank, credit card, mortgage, insurance, retailers, Web sites, subscriptions—you have a privacy agreement with virtually every organization and institution to whom you provide personal information. If you haven't physically opted out, you automatically opted in, which means you gave these companies permission to traffic in your confidential information!

Make a List

Opting out takes time. Don't let it frustrate you. You can't do it overnight, but if you do it methodically, it requires less time than you might imagine. Make a list. Each time you receive a bill, catalog, or magazine; log on to a Web site; or get solicited by a company you've done business with, add that company's name to your list and then opt out of their privacy agreement. Take out your wallet and make a note of all the companies with whom you have confidential relationships—credit cards, banks, insurance carriers, auto clubs, gas stations, discount clubs, supermarkets, health clubs, chain stores—and add their names to your list. Then opt out of their privacy agreements, one by one.

It's all or nothing; you can't opt out halfway! What's to stop companies from whom you don't opt out from sharing your information with others? As I noted previously, once information is in the public domain, it's out there in perpetuity! Once your information is out there, your only viable option is to manage it. You can't put the toothpaste back in the tube, but you can screw the cap back on by opting out!

Logic would dictate that the opt-out procedure is ass-backwards, and it is! A company should be required to obtain your explicit permission—in other words, have you *opt in*—before harvesting, selling, or trafficking in your personal information. But the unfortunate truth is our laws have not kept pace with the deployment of technology because laws are revolutionary and technology is evolutionary. New legislation takes time and leaves upheaval in its wake. Technology develops moment to moment and advances every day.

There's a second, more nefarious reason why the opt-in/opt-out procedure is ass-backwards. As Tip O'Neill used to say, "money is the mother's milk of politics." The information, technology, and media conglomerates form a powerful information lobby that contributes freely to the slush fund of any politician willing to vote their way. Until legislation is passed that protects the average citizen from the information vultures in our society, the onus is on individuals to opt out on their own!

The top 20 political contributors in the technology/media sector appear in the following table. Do you notice any patterns? I profile Steve Kirsch, the founder of Propel Software, in Chapter 5, which is about junk faxes. Steve is a well-known philanthropist and privacy advocate, as you'll see. His political contributions, primarily to liberal Democrats, were altruistic. I don't believe that's the case with many of these other conglomerates, however. Buying congressional votes is their prime motivation because all have a vested interest in harvesting our personal information. Note that WorldCom and Global Crossing have both gone belly-up despite their million-dollar political contributions.

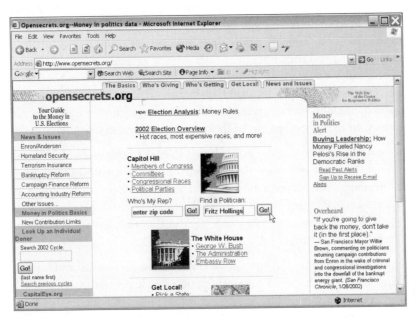

Figure 3.10 *OpenSecrets.org*

Top 2002 Political Contributors in the Technology and Media Sectors

Rank	Computer/ Internet: $18,247,505	Communications: $77,244,271	Movies/Television/ Music: $29,373,492
1	Propel: $3,364,036	Saban Entertainment: $7,782,000	Saban Entertainment: $7,782,000
2	Microsoft: $2,955,028	Shangri-La Entertainment: $6,580,000	Shangri-La Entertainment: $6,580,000
3	Affiliated Computer Services: $524,058	Propel: $3,364,036	AOL Time Warner: $1,169,894
4	EDS Corp: $482,868	Microsoft: $2,955,028	Walt Disney Co: $991,039
5	Gateway: $396,527	SBC Communications: $2,598,875	Vivendi Universal: $809,365
6	Oracle: $387,834	AT&T: $2,259,881	Chartwell Partners: $762,000
7	Cisco: $376,548	BellSouth: $2,110,835	Cablevision: $611,085
8	Siebel: $324,749	Verizon: $1,913,341	National Association of Broadcasters: $601,851
9	Collazo: $242,810	Loral Communications: $1,768,300	National Cable & Telecommunications Association: $483,930
10	Kirchman: $241,404	Newsweb: $1,763,000	Sillerman Companies: $471,099
11	Gen3: $237,000	AOL Time Warner: $1,461,644	News Corp: $463,587
12	AOL Time Warner: $236,000	Global Crossing: $1,214,670	Recording Industry of America: $425,319
13	OmniSky Inc: $235,000	WorldCom: $1,040,964	Viacom Inc: $407,882
14	Intuit Inc: $225,775	Walt Disney: $995,709	Comcast: $393,872

Top 2002 Political Contributors in the Technology and Media Sectors—continued

15	eBay, Inc: $207,250	Qwest Communications: $922,145	Hubbard Broadcasting: $326,750
16	Intel: $204,658	Vivendi Universal: $834,815	West Grand Media: $313,000
17	Learning Co: $194,000	Chartwell Partners: $762,000	Jovon Broadcasting: $275,000
18	VeriSign: $159,467	Echostar: $655,750	Charter Communications: $246,930
19	Escription: $154,000	Cablevision: $611,085	Bresnan: $239,750
20	Dell: $138,749	National Association of Broadcasters: $601,851	King World Productions: $239,000

Source: Center for Responsive Politics/OpenSecrets.org

Practicing Stealth

I asked my mother if she knew what a privacy agreement was. She said, "Sure, I get them in the mail all the time." I asked her what she did with them, and she replied, "I rip them up and throw them away! What do you think I do?"

Practicing stealth is like opting out—you can't do it halfway. Stealth is invisibility! Just as a firewall makes your computer invisible to others on the network, practicing stealth puts a virtual firewall between you and those who would invade your privacy. You take vitamins to fortify your health. Fortify your privacy by practicing stealth!

The best way to practice stealth is follow the two Golden Rules. When it comes to providing personal information:

When in doubt, leave it out!

When it comes to privacy agreements:

Always opt out!

And don't forget:

Use your digital doppelganger!

CHAPTER 4
Convergence

Everything Is Wired to Everything

> ➤ **How a Simple Coupon Can Lead to**
>   **Your Worst Nightmare**

In a word, this book is about convergence. Convergence is the next killer app! Convergence means different things to different people, which is why it has become such a popular buzzword. My definition of convergence is very simple:

Everything is wired to everything!

This means your television, telephone, cell phone, fax machine, satellite dish, mailbox, computer, PDA, e-mail, ISP, Web browser, cable box, Xbox, lunch box, TiVo, SUV, wallet, and God only knows what else are all wired to a supercomputer that keeps track of your every move! Convergence permeates everything. It is the bastard child of advertising and technology. It was born of fear and confusion. I wrote about convergence in my last book before I even knew what it was called.

I had just attended the Internet World trade show. It was the spring of 2000, the last gasp of the dot-com boom, although nobody knew it yet.

"What planet is this," thought I to myself, as I wandered down the aisle in the first of several huge exhibit halls. This was the biggest, splashiest, richest computer show this side of COMDEX, and I couldn't figure out what the hell half of these companies were selling. I was somewhat relieved to discover many of the exhibitors themselves couldn't explain what they were selling!

It took me a little while to figure it out, but now I know. They were selling convergence! Technology designed to spy on us, predict our needs, and fulfill our fantasies by selling us the appropriate products. Marketers want to march into our living rooms like some digital Dutch uncles and tell us what to buy. This is no news flash. Advertising has always pushed our buttons to sell us products. What's new is the implementation of converging technologies that spy on us as a marketing tool! Advertising, or "badvertising," as I call it, is turning each and every one of us into a human cookie!

How a Simple Coupon Can Lead to Your Worst Nightmare

Suppose a new Pizza Palace opens in your neighborhood. They want your business, and you receive a coupon addressed to "Occupant" for a large "That's Amore" pizza with three toppings for only $10.99. It's such an appetizing deal that you pick up the phone and place an order. Gotcha! Before the clerk utters a word, your name and phone number are trapped in the Pizza Palace caller ID system. What's the first thing they ask? Name and phone number, please. At this point Pizza Palace already knows this information, but they're qualifying you, checking you out! They don't want their delivery people going on any wild goose chases, or worse, getting mugged or ripped off. In other words, they're qualifying you to protect themselves, which is understandable.

Figure 4.1 *Pizza coupons*

What's the next thing they ask? Address, apartment number, and security code, please. The clerk is no slouch when it comes to typing. It's the main qualification that earned him the job. He inputs your information into their computer database. This will save time the next time you order because you're only a mouse-click away, a convenience for both Pizza Palace and you. At this stage in the transaction you finally place the order, charge it to your credit card, and if all goes well, a piping hot "That's Amore" pizza arrives at your front door half an hour later.

When the Moon Hits Your I.D. Like a Big Pizza Pie

Chew on this! You just sacrificed your privacy to get a pizza delivered for $3 off. Your metamorphosis from anonymous occupant to identifiable customer took less than a minute and was entirely subconscious. And you provided much more than your name, phone number, address, and credit card info. Your order reveals a lot about you. Are you a vegetarian or do you eat meat? Is your fridge stocked with drinks or did you go for a two-liter Pepsi? Do you live alone? Have a family? How many pizzas did you order? Do you have a sweet tooth? You ordered a "Frozone Calzone" for dessert, didn't you? An airbrushed coupon triggered a Pavlovian response that prompted you to pick up the phone and provide private information to a perfect stranger.

I told you, you're a Manchurian candidate! Your personal information is being harvested without you even knowing it. You're being profiled and targeted! That's why you received the "Occupant" coupon in the first place. Everything there is to know about you already exists on that supercomputer I told you about, and each time you add to your trail of digital breadcrumbs, the supercomputer processes and updates your profile. Pizza Palace sells the information it gathers about you back to the company that sold it your mailing address! That's the way the information business works.

Today, an innocuous coupon is a high-tech marketing gimmick designed to trick people into exchanging personal information for a negligible benefit. Coupons and their cousin, chain-store discount cards, track what products and brands people buy, where and when they shop, and how much they spend. Marketers use this information to profile each customer's personality and buying patterns. They then target that individual with personalized advertising and sell the profiles to other companies, who in turn do the same thing, over and over again. The information industry is playing Three-Card Monte with our privacy!

Low-Tech Convergence

The implementation of convergence is a relatively recent phenomenon, and the evolution is ongoing. Low-tech intrusions, like the pizza coupon, pose a more insidious threat to our privacy than the high-tech variety because we were taught to trust low technology. Not long ago I got a telemarketing phone call that illustrates this.

I had just bit the bullet and gone broadband. Cable modem, digital cable—"The Works!" as Adelphia, my scandal-ridden cable company, calls it. Five minutes after saying goodbye to the cable installer, my phone rang.

> *Weber:* Hello?
>
> *Telemarketer:* Mr. Weber, this is Wally Loman from Adelphia Communications. Pardon the intrusion, but I'm calling to see how the installation went.
>
> *Weber:* Fine, thanks.
>
> *Loman:* Mr. Weber, do you happen to have a pencil handy?

Harry Houdini called this technique "misdirection."

> *Weber:* For what?
>
> *Loman:* You might want to jot down my employee I.D. number. It's badge 07295-B, as in boy.

Figure 4.2 *Adelphia homepage*

Weber (impatient): Would you mind telling me what this call is in reference to?

Loman: Our partner, TV Guide, wants to send you eight free editions of its digital cable guide at no cost or obligation. We want you to experience the full spectrum of benefits digital cable offers. It's our gift to you. Are you interested?

I usually don't engage telemarketers, but this guy was so slick I went along with him.

Weber: Sure. What do I have to lose?

Loman: Mr. Weber, without your objection I'd like to record the remainder of this conversation for record-keeping purposes. In a moment, Ms. Finkle, my sales associate, will join us on the line. That's spelled F-I-N-K-L-E.

The short hairs on my neck rose.

Weber: I don't give a damn how you spell Finkle! Stop. I object!

Loman (persistent): What do you object to, sir?

Weber: I object to having my conversation recorded, and I object to you turning a sales pitch into a mock legal deposition! You and I both know every word you just uttered was scripted.

Loman: It isn't necessary to record the conversation if it makes you uncomfortable, Mr. Weber.

Weber: Listen! I want my name removed from all mailing and phone lists. I'm opting out! Do you understand me?

Loman: Yes sir. I'll put you on our "don't call" list right away. Sorry to bother you, Mr. Weber. Have a nice day.

This is a scary conversation when you break it down. What prompted my phone to ring in the first place? Convergence! The same Adelphia computer that activated my digital cable notified another computer in some remote telemarketing boiler room to put me in their sales queue. TV Guide paid Adelphia for my account information. Odds are if I had swallowed the bait, I wouldn't have canceled after eight issues, and TV Guide would have a new subscriber. I didn't bite. The question remains, what will the telemarketing company do with my personal information? Around and around it goes, where it stops nobody knows. Once information is out there, it's out there in perpetuity!

I call Wally Loman the "Telemarketer from Hell" because he was such a slick professional. He's a "closer." Had I consented to have the conversation recorded—an outrageous sales ploy and an invasion of privacy by any standard—Ms. Finkle, an "order taker," would have wrapped up the loose ends, liberating Wally to charm the next prospect.

It's no accident that Wally did a complete 180 the minute I asked to be removed from the list. It's the law. In 1991, President Bush signed the Telephone Consumer Protection Act (TCPA). Public Law 102-243 (1991) amended Title II of the Communications Act of 1934 by adding a new section, 47 U.S.C. Section 227, enacted by Congress to "reduce the nuisance and invasion of privacy caused by telemarketing and prerecorded calls."

If you tell a telemarketer to take your name off their list, that organization is required by Federal law to put your number on their "don't call" list and keep it in their database for ten years.

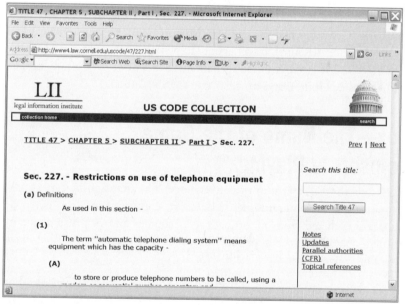

Figure 4.3 *Telephone Consumer Protection Act Section 227*

Listless

Unfortunately, opting out doesn't always work. It simply puts you on another list—a company's "don't call" list. The problem is you're already on hundreds of lists! The word "list" in this context is a throwback to the sixties, when the number of people a marketer could contact was so small that the names could be kept on a sheet of paper. Today marketing companies have huge databases containing every bit of information ever collected on an individual. That database is available to authorized users such as subscribers, as well as unauthorized users such as hackers! Because every phone number in the world can now be stored on a PC's hard drive, and most can be purchased inexpensively on CD-ROM, your best option is to have your name marked as a "don't call."

A decade ago, software came on floppy disks; computer viruses, spam, and Internet fraud were unheard of; and private information was relatively secure. The good old days are gone! Today, conglomerates like Microsoft and AOL package entertainment and technology designed to hijack our privacy by entwining our lifestyles, properties, and finances. They want to be one-stop shops. If Bill Gates has his way, one day Microsoft will be your bank (.NET Passport Wallet/Palladium), travel agent (Expedia), phone company (bCentral Wireless), ISP (MSN), news channel (MSNBC), real estate broker (MSN House & Home), and car salesman (MSN Autos).

Xbox—The Name of the Game Microsoft Is Playing

Bill Gates is the P.T. Barnum of convergence! The question is, can an all-encompassing conglomerate like Microsoft compartmentalize personal information gathered from a cornucopia of sources and be trusted not to commingle it and abuse our privacy? Let's look at one Microsoft product spawned by convergence.

The very name Xbox reeks of convergence. Xbox is a gaming console that consists of a hard drive, a CD-ROM, an NVIDIA 3D graphics controller, RAM, a modem, and an Intel CPU. In other words, Xbox is a personal computer equipped with an operating system that plays games. Hackers have already managed to turn Xboxes into Linux computers, but that's beside the point. It was predictable! By the time you read this, I'm sure there will be Wintel hacks as well.

Microsoft is burning cash on Xbox! It doesn't take an MBA from Harvard to tell you that will happen when you sell a souped-up computer for $199. Most analysts estimate that Microsoft lost $125 to $150 per Xbox before slashing $100 off the $299 retail price early in 2003. That means Microsoft is currently losing $225 to $250 on each sale. Add to that the $2 billon budget John O'Rourke, marketing director of Microsoft's Games division, estimates the company will spend over the next five years to make Xbox the leading video game console. If Microsoft sells 11 million units as predicted, it will lose approximately $4.5 billion—almost 12 percent of the $38 billion mountain of cash it took the company 25 years to amass. Is Bill Gates crazy, or crazy like a fox? It depends who you ask.

Bill Gates will tell you Xbox fits into Microsoft's overall online subscription strategy. Microsoft currently sells a $49.95 add-on package, Xbox Live, which includes a 12-month Internet subscription to the service and a headset microphone that connects to Xbox for real-time voice chat. This fee doesn't include a broadband connection, which is required.

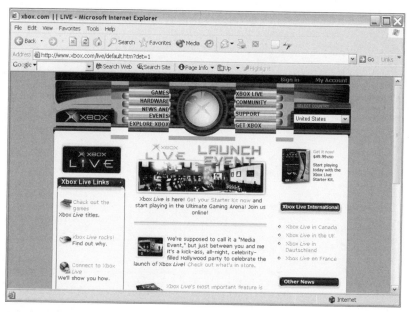

Figure 4.4 *Xbox Live Web site*

Market analysts will tell you Microsoft can afford to give away the hardware because the games are selling so well—an average of 4.1 software titles for every Xbox sold. Matt Rosoff, a research analyst at Direction on Microsoft, explains that "the profit is really driven by the games in this business. In selling Xbox, Microsoft is installing sockets into which they can sell more games."

Sony will tell you Microsoft is giving away Xbox to kill the competition, their PlayStation 2.

Conspiracy theorists will tell you there's a chip in Xbox that beams your activities back to Microsoft.

Take your pick. Personally, I think Bill Gates wants a Microsoft box attached to every television set that is in turn connected to the Internet. Adding a TV tuner to Xbox would cost around 20 bucks and convert Xbox into a full-blown "delivery on demand" set-top receiver. The point is Microsoft isn't just a software company anymore and the reason for that is convergence. Bill Gates is willing to lose money on Xbox now because he has always gambled on the future.

CHAPTER 5

Tactical and Practical Digital Defense (Part 1)

The $2.2 Trillion Fax

➢ **Turnabout Is Fair Play**

➢ **Resourcefulness**

➢ **"Do Not Call" List Update**

Steve Kirsch is a living legend in Silicon Valley. As the founder of three high-tech companies with a combined market cap of more than $5 billion, Kirsch's biggest business coup was selling Infoseek, his Internet search portal, to the Walt Disney Company in November, 1999—at the height of the dot-com bubble. Although Kirsch is a millionaire many times over, he's perhaps best known for being an activist and philanthropist. He and his wife, Michelle, have donated more than $5 million to educational causes through the Kirsch Foundation, established in 1999. Kirsch was ranked number 8 on Slate's 60 largest American charitable contributions of 1999, and he was named one of the top 10 entrepreneurs of 2000 by *Red Herring* magazine. Even with all these accomplishments under his belt, Steve Kirsch may go down in history for what he did in the summer of 2002, when he filed one of the largest civil suits in American jurisprudence—an unprecedented $2.2 trillion class action suit.

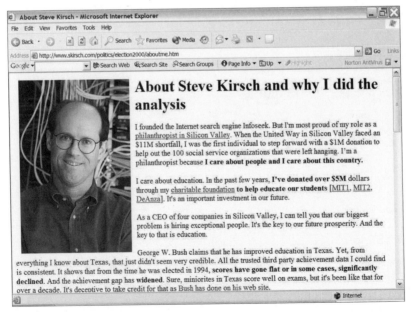

Figure 5.1 *Steve Kirsch Web site*

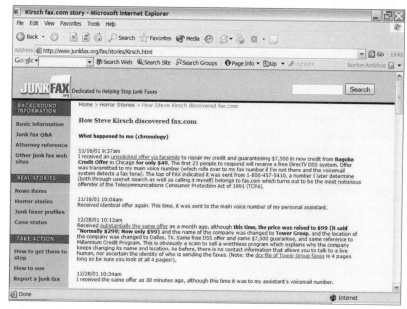

Figure 5.2 *http://www.junkfax.org/fax/stories/kirsch.html*

Here's Kirsch's story in his own words, edited for the sake of brevity. The full account appears on his Web site, at http://www.junkfax.org.

HOW I DISCOVERED FAX.COM

By Steve Kirsch

Chronology

11/16/01 9:37 a.m.

I received an unsolicited offer via facsimile at my company headquarters to repair my credit, guaranteeing $7,500 in new credit from Bagoba Credit Offer in Chicago for only $49. The offer was transmitted to my main voice number (which rolls over to my fax number if I'm not there and the voicemail system detects a fax tone). The top of the fax indicated it was sent from 1-800-457-5410, a number I later determined (both through a USENET search and by calling it myself) belongs to fax.com, the most notorious offender of the Telecommunications Consumer Protection Act of 1991 (TCPA).

11/16/01 10:04 a.m.

Received the identical offer again. This time, it was sent to the main voice number of my personal assistant.

12/28/01 10:12 a.m.

I received substantially the same offer as a month ago, although this time the price was raised to $99, and the name of the company was changed to Tower Group. The location of the company was changed to Dallas, TX, but it included the same free DSS offer, the same $7,500 guarantee, and the same reference to the Millennium Credit Program. This is obviously a scam to sell a worthless program, which explains why the company keeps changing its name and location. As before, there was no contact information to allow you to talk to a live human or ascertain the identity of the sender.

12/28/01 10:34 a.m.

I received the same offer as 30 minutes ago, although this time it was to my assistant's voicemail number.

1/5/02 2:00 p.m.

I decided to take a closer look at the other faxes and look up who each 800 number belonged to. I did a Google groups search and found the revealing posting shown in the following figure. Things were starting to make sense to me.

I later determined that there were a variety of 800 numbers for removal printed on the fax, but that five of them were all owned by the same company: fax.com. Twenty-two faxes and five different removal numbers

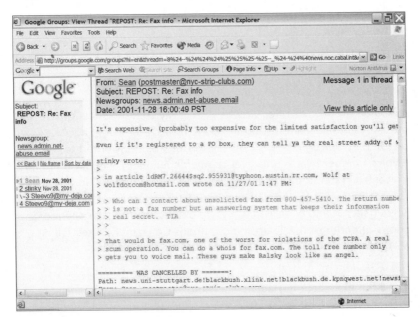

Figure 5.3 *Google Fax.com post*

over the past four months, just to me! What's even more irritating is that there is absolutely no way for most normal people to figure out who sent the fax or who owns the 800 number because phone companies do not disclose this information for privacy reasons, and if you dial the fax.com removal number, they do not identify the company. There is also no station ID used by the sender's fax machine. However, by using my investigative tools, I was able to confirm that all the 800 numbers listed on these faxes did, in fact, point to the same place, namely, fax.com. I've discovered only 10 popular fax.com removal numbers, but they have 23 toll-free numbers, so this is only one-third of the numbers they use.

Table 5.1 Steve Kirsch's Tools for Investigating Junk Faxes

Site	URL
Junkfaxes.org	http://www.junkfaxes.com
FCC Telecommunications Consumers Division—TCPA Actions	http://www.fcc.gov/eb/tcd/ufax.html
Geektools	http://www.geektools.com
Docusearch Investigations	http://www.docusearch.com/index.html
Cell Phone Magic	http://www.cell-phone-numbers.com
US Search	http://www.ussearch.com/wlcs/index.jsp
Reverse Address Directory	http://www.reverseaddress.com
Craig Ball's Sampler of Informal Discovery Links	http://www.craigball.com/hotlinks.html
KnowX.com	http://www.knowx.com
ScreenNow	http://www.screennow.com
Net Detective	http://ndet.jeanharris.com
OnlineDetective	http://www.onlinedetective.com
SuperPages.com	http://www.superpages.com
GNU wget	http://www.gnu.org/software/wget/wget.html
Trash Archaeology and FloridaDetectives.com	http://www.floridadetectives.com/art_dumpster.htm
Officers.com Electronics and Surveillance	http://www.officer.com/prodsur.htm
CCS International Ltd.	http://www.spyzone.com

Fax Removal Numbers

If you ever get a fax with one of these removal numbers, it means you've probably been spammed by fax.com.

- 800-443-7620 (now disconnected)
- 800-443-7628
- 800-457-5410 (also used as a "from" number on some faxes)
- 800-663-8758
- 800-766-0816
- 800-785-6698
- 800-822-9033
- 800-965-7235
- 800-976-3734
- 800-992-5329

I spent time looking up the business address of each fax with a fax.com removal number. Doing a bit of detective work on the Internet, I was able to get contact information for virtually all of the companies that used fax.com to send me unsolicited faxes that I saved. I then compiled profiles of all these companies, including their contact information and judgments against them, on a single Web page for easy Internet identification.

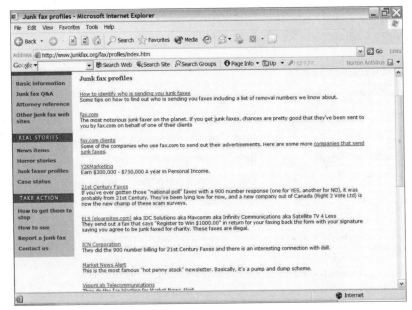

Figure 5.4 *Junkfax.org—fax company profiles*

1/11/02 10:00 a.m.

I got the Tower Group offer again. Two copies! Traced these calls to Robert B. He must be the local agent for fax.com (fax.com has various satellite locations doing dialing for them).

5/12/02 and 5/13/02

My company was war-dialed from San Jose: 408-937-6725, 408-937-6771, 408-937-6459. Everyone at work was left a fax tone on their voicemail. For more details on this war-dialer location, see fax.com.

Junk Fax Evidence

- ➤ Tower Group/Bagoba Credit: Four faxes to repair my credit
- ➤ Misc: 22 faxes sent to me from fax.com (from 11 clients)
- ➤ y2marketing: Three faxes sent within one hour to me on 1/6/02
- ➤ 21st Century (the 900 yes/no poll question)
- ➤ 21st Century: Three faxes
- ➤ Market News Alert
- ➤ Market News Alert: Eight faxes
- ➤ Wall Street Watch (10/23/01)
- ➤ Copiers Direct (no header at all; sent in q4 2001)
- ➤ Quality Reprographics (8/30/01)
- ➤ Central Imaging (1/7/02)

Fax.com Violations

- ➤ They sent unsolicited faxes.
- ➤ They didn't remove me when I asked. Even after I received e-mail from them confirming that I was removed, I got three faxes a few days later! I don't think they remove anyone. They just used a different 800 removal number to make it look like I popped up on a new list. However, this means by not removing people, they are racking up their "unsolicited" points.
- ➤ Their fax headers don't comply with the law because they don't identify the name and phone number of the sender (i.e., their client) in the top or bottom margin.
- ➤ I can't do anything about this, but under 47 U.S.C. § 227(f)(1) the California State Attorney General can sue fax.com for both technical violations and unsolicited faxes, enjoin them from making any more calls into California, and also get treble damages as well.

These Faxes Were Unsolicited

1. I never give out my main voice number to use as a fax.
2. My assistant never gives out her voice number to use as a fax.
3. No one in our household has any need for credit repair.
4. No one has a prior business relationship with either Bagoba or Tower Group.

In fact, there is no known way to speak with these businesses even if you want to establish a relationship. I've never had a credit problem, and the offer transmitted to me indicates a complete lack of any knowledge about me. Anyone with only a passing knowledge of our household knows that we would never be interested in such an offer.

We'd never give out our voice numbers to be used by fax machines because these numbers are all normally answered by humans (except at night or when we are out of the house, when an answering machine comes on, but it can automatically transfer fax calls to our fax machine). It would be quite obnoxious to answer the phone and hear a fax tone. That is why we have and always use a dedicated fax number—a fax number which apparently never made it into the fax.com database.

Nor would we ever intentionally enter our voice numbers into the fax.com database. Indeed, fax.com seems to have all our voice numbers, but not our dedicated fax number.

Therefore, the only way for fax.com to have gotten those phone numbers is by using a computerized dialer known as a "war dialer" (since any human dialer would have recognized that these were normally voice lines). They have been known to do this, and were in fact cited for exactly this offense by Washington State.

How is it possible that virtually all the unsolicited faxes I get are from fax.com? That 11 different companies have faxed me and they all use fax.com? That I've never heard of these companies before? That some of them didn't even exist a few months ago? That all of them are faxing to my voice numbers instead of my fax number?

And why does fax.com have at least 23 different removal numbers? Why not just one, if they have nothing to hide? And why does the removal number change when the client sends a new fax? For example, the *Wall Street Examiner* sent me a fax with an 800-443-7628 removal number, but the removal number listed on the fax that Junkfax.org received just 60 days earlier is 800-766-0816. Both numbers still work.

And why don't fax.com machines identify themselves (SenderID field during the handshake)? Why doesn't fax.com identify itself anywhere on the fax or at any place when you call the removal number?

The fax.com Web site blatantly brags about their database: "fax.com has identified over 30 million untouched fax numbers." They offer to send faxes to their database or yours. It's blatantly illegal to make such an offer. See excerpts from their Web site for more on this illegal practice. Finally, they have been cited in Usenet postings as being the most notorious abuser of the TCPA.

Why I'm Bringing Suit

I have one goal and one goal only. I want this practice stopped. I'm tired of the fax calls waking us up. I'm tired of saying "hello" to a fax tone. I'm doing this for me and for everyone else. Clearly, despite six separate citations by the FCC in the past 12 months (they've been cited more than any other company, at an average rate of one citation a month in the first half of 2001) and a settlement agreement with Washington State, fax.com continues to send facsimiles to numbers belonging to those individuals who have no previous business relationship with their client. I want this practice to end. Not just for fax.com, but for everyone engaging in this practice. And I'm willing to (and can afford to) spend whatever it takes to make sure this happens. I want the law enforced.

I have no monetary motivation to bring this suit. In fact, I'll probably lose money because any settlement will likely go to a charitable foundation to

➤ Fund the legal pursuit of other offenders.

➤ Educate the public on how to pursue offenders.

From a legal viewpoint, our case is completely airtight (even though there are judges here and there who misinterpret the law). There is no escape. Every possible defense has been tried and failed. (It's just a matter of time before a California court sees through the current "opt out" defense.) That is why Hooters was slapped with a $12 million damage award, and why the Dallas Cowboys recently settled. I've detailed all the possible legal defenses, and I explain why they will fail.

So fax.com will lose. They will be put out of business permanently. Plus, all their clients will be forced to pay up to the maximum restitution as provided by law and/or declare bankruptcy. If this doesn't dry up the supply and demand for this illegal practice, I will continue to file lawsuits against these companies and their clients until it does. Hopefully, this $2.2 trillion class action lawsuit alone will get people's attention, and the practice will stop. I have no interest in spending my time filing lawsuits, but if that's what it takes, so be it. The first judgment we win will fund future lawsuits so that the junk faxers will be financing their own demise.

Why $2.2 Trillion?

The reason for the $2.2 trillion is that fax.com sends out three to four million faxes a day. They've been in business at least three years; do the math. It's more than $500 billion per year. My guess is that the actual statutory remedy is many times that amount. In my case, I receive about one fax every two days from fax.com at my home. In short, fax.com sends out 1,000 linear feet of faxes per day. That's further than most of us can hit a golf ball. It's 6,000 reams of paper or $60,000 per day in paper expenses for the recipients. We estimate that when you add up everything, it's over $100 million in expenses that are pushed off to the recipients (about 10 cents per page).

Wish me luck!

Steve Kirsch

On August 23, 2002, a coalition of California activists led by Steve Kirsch filed a jaw-dropping $2.2 trillion set of lawsuits against fax.com, its advertisers, and Cox Business Services (its telecommunications provider). The multiple suits, filed in both California state and federal courts, seek class action status and punitive damages. Kirsch claimed, "The right to free speech stops at my front door. You are not allowed to invade my privacy and use my resources to send me your messages! Millions of junk faxes are clogging the nation's fax machines, jamming communications, and possibly endangering lives."

Turnabout Is Fair Play

What would compel someone to operate a company that profits from invading the privacy of others? I contacted Kevin Katz, fax.com's president, to air his company's side of the story for the record. The first time we touched base Kevin was on the road. He returned my call from his hotel room in St. Louis, where he was appearing as a witness on behalf of fax.com in yet another lawsuit—an FCC-proposed $5.38 million fine against fax.com for faxing unsolicited advertisements. Katz was testifying before Missouri's Eighth Circuit Court, and he warily admitted that if the FCC won this one, it would be the largest fine ever imposed by the government for such a violation. By his own admission, Katz has spent as much time in court lately as in his offices overlooking the bay in Aliso Viejo, California. And with Kirsch's unprecedented lawsuit looming, the future of fax.com sometimes appears bleak. But Katz makes no bones about it; he believes the right to free speech as defined by the First Amendment of the Constitution will protect fax.com in these lawsuits.

Katz, who speaks with a cordial South African dialect, is obviously beleaguered by the considerable legal flak surrounding him and his enterprise—

which isn't to imply that he doesn't deserve it. Before talking to me, he wanted my assurance that I wasn't working for Steve Kirsch. I explained that I stumbled upon Kirsch's $2.2 trillion lawsuit while doing research for a book about privacy, and I wanted to include fax.com's side of the story. He then opened up. I found Katz to be charming, but also mercurial and hard to pin down. Take his company's Web site, for example (see the following figure).

The Fax.com Web Site

I thought I typed the wrong URL the first time I surfed over to fax.com. It appeared to be a child advocacy site for missing children; a network called the Internet Emergency Response Network that specializes in faxing Amber Alerts for missing kids.

Figure 5.5 *Fax.com's missing-child home page*

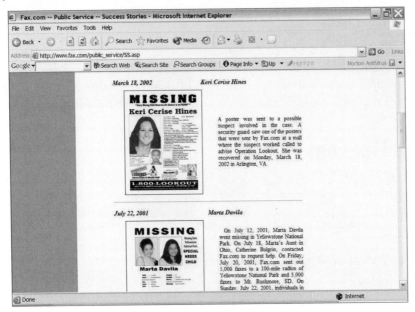

Figure 5.6 *Fax.com's second missing-children page*

I clicked on Enter Site and was directed to a second page containing eight more missing-children fax posters. The Web site was beginning to remind me of one of the fake building façades on a Hollywood back lot.

I clicked Home on the second page and was finally directed to fax.com's Targeted Marketing Solutions page, which contains the nuts and bolts of fax.com's business. Its mission statement reads

> Fax.com broadcast faxing allows you to send a high volume of fax information to hundreds, thousands, or even millions of recipients. You get high delivery rates, immediate reporting of successful and unsuccessful faxes, and unparalleled customer service.

The first question I asked Katz was what was up with his Web site. Was it a PR ploy? Or was he perhaps trying to qualify fax.com as a nonprofit organization to slip through some legal loophole? He emphatically insisted that this was not the case. Katz portrayed fax.com as a civic-minded organization that was instrumental in helping to locate nine missing children. That was the company line—that faxes somehow serve the public good. Then Katz tried to put words in my mouth. "I'm sure you've received unsolicited fax material that you've benefited from," he insisted. I informed Katz that he was mistaken, and I told him my fax story to illustrate my point.

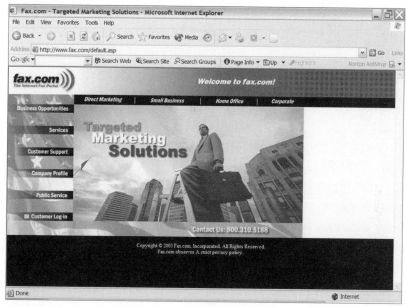

Figure 5.7 *Fax.com's Targeted Marketing Solutions page*

My Fax Story

A stack of junk faxes two feet high greeted me upon my return from an extended vacation. Ads for inkjet cartridges and toner, Wall Street penny stock newsletters, vacation timeshares—the same type of crap Steve Kirsch was getting. And I did the same thing Kirsch did; dialed a bunch of fax removal numbers that were either disconnected or eternally busy. The junk faxes didn't stop either. I was getting one or two a day and growing increasingly frustrated. I confess—I even called a few voice numbers listed on fax paper bought with my hard-earned money and cursed out the telemarketers on the other end. Nothing seemed to help. The junk faxes just kept coming!

When I first moved into my home 16 years ago, I had two land lines installed with phone numbers that were one digit apart. Over the years, the second land line has served as a combination private number, second incoming line, dedicated fax number, and dedicated line for a dial-up modem. But time marches on! My cell phone now serves as a private line, and I use a broadband cable modem for Internet access. Without my realizing it, my second land line had become obsolete. The only purpose the second line now served was to deliver these annoying junk faxes!

Necessity is the mother of invention. By pulling the plug on the second number I not only got even with the lowlifes who had the gall to spam me—I knocked 32 percent off my monthly telecommunications budget! After relating my story to Kevin Katz I asked him some pointed questions.

1. Do you ever receive unsolicited faxes for products in which you have no interest?

2. How do people get on a "do not call" list?

3. Why are most "do not call" lists so ineffective? Why hasn't fax.com developed a foolproof "do not call" list?

4. Aren't unsolicited faxes illegal under the 47 U.S.C. § 227(b)(1)(C) and U.S.C. § 552(a)(e)(3)?

5. What are your thoughts on Steve Kirsch's $2.2 trillion lawsuit against fax.com? What do you predict the disposition will be?

Before responding, Katz wanted to review the questions with his attorney. I agreed to e-mail him a Q&A. A month passed, and I placed a follow-up phone call. Katz called me back from his office, where he was on a speakerphone with his attorney. I gathered from the lawyer's questions that he didn't want Kevin to cooperate. I left the door open, but that's the last I heard from him.

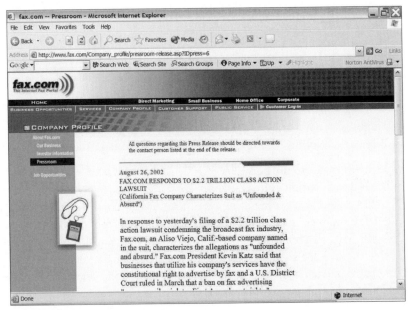

Figure 5.8 *Fax.com's response to the lawsuit*

Legal Update—March 21, 2003

A federal appeals court ruled that a law restricting junk faxes was constitutional, setting a precedent that favors legal attempts to restrict unsolicited e-mail as well. The Eighth Circuit Court of Appeals reversed a lower court's ruling, concluding that a 1991 federal law banning unsolicited fax advertising did not violate the First Amendment's guarantee of freedom of expression. This is the case in which Katz was defending fax.com when he first phoned me from his hotel room in Missouri. By his own admission, this defeat was a crushing blow. One press report read, "Fax.com could not be reached for comment. A spokesman said the company shut down early on Friday because of the U.S. war against Iraq." The statement reminded me of fax.com's missing children Web pages. Katz can drape his company in red, white, and blue all he wants, but without the shield of the First Amendment to hide behind, fax.com is well on its way to becoming an endangered species. The wheels of justice grind slowly. By the time Steve Kirsch's lawsuit wends its way through the court system, fax.com could be out of business. If it isn't, I pity Kevin Katz. Steve Kirsch is one dude I wouldn't want to mess with!

Resourcefulness

Outrage is an invaluable tool when you know how to channel your anger. Steve Kirsch used technology to turn the tables on the technology that victimized and offended him. He may have more money than you and I, but the resources he used to do his research are free—the Internet, his brains, and elbow grease! The next time you're victimized, you can do the same. Learn a lesson from Steve Kirsch. Surf to each Web site cited in Table 5.1. Create an Investigation Tools folder on your Favorites menu, and then bookmark each site.

At the very least, learn a lesson from me. Are you paying for telephone numbers, utilities, ISPs, or other services that have become obsolete? Take inventory and pull the plug on any services you don't need. Each time you do, you invariably pull the plug on one more source of unsolicited spam, telemarketing calls, and junk faxes—and you'll save some money to boot!

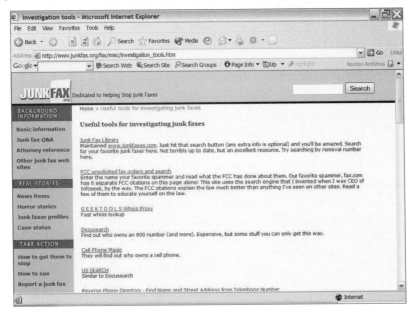

Figure 5.9 *Steve Kirsch's investigative tools*

"Do Not Call" List Update

According to the Federal Trade Commission, their amended TSR (*Telemarketing Sales Rule*) will put consumers in charge of the number of telemarketing calls they receive at home. By creating a national "do not call" registry, the FTC will make it easier and more efficient for consumers to stop getting unwanted telemarketing sales calls.

The National "Do Not Call" Registry Is Online!

In July 2003, consumers began registering for the national "do not call" registry online at (http://donotcall.gov/). Two million people registered the first day! Why don't you put down this book right now and register? Simply log-on or call 888-382-1222 from the phone number you want to register. In September, 2003, telemarketers and other sellers will have access to the registry. They will be required to scrub their call lists against the national "do not call" registry at least once every 90 days.

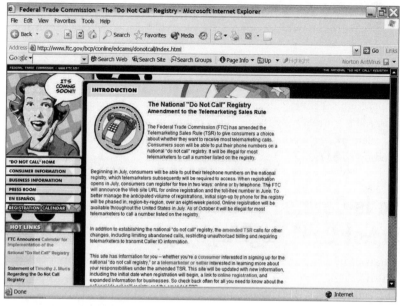

Figure 5.10 *National "do not call" list site*

In October, 2003, the FCC and each state will start to enforce the national "do not call" registry provisions of the amended TSR. Violators are subject to a fine of up to $11,000 per violation. At this point, consumers on the registry should start to get fewer telemarketing calls.

Don't allow the late breaking legal wrangling to dissuade you from registering for the National Do Not Call list. When the smoke clears—and you can be sure it will because President Bush, Congress, the FTC, and the FCC have all interceded on the consumer's behalf—you'll be one of the 50 million plus Americans who reap the immediate benefits.

How Does the National "Do Not Call" Registry Work?

If you register by phone, you will have to call from the telephone number that you wish to register. If you register online, you may need to provide limited personal information for confirmation. The only identifying information that will be kept in the registry will be the phone number you register. You can expect fewer calls within three months of signing up for the registry.

Your number will stay in the registry for five years or until you remove it or change phone numbers. After five years, you will be able to renew your registration.

The law requires telemarketers to search the registry every 90 days and delete phone numbers on the registry from their call lists. If you find that you are receiving telemarketing calls even after you register your telephone number, you can file a complaint with the FTC online or by calling a toll-free number. A telemarketer who disregards the national "do not call" registry could be fined up to $11,000 for each call.

Who Is Covered by the National "Do Not Call" Registry?

Placing your number on the national "do not call" registry will stop most (but not all) telemarketing calls. Some businesses are exempt from the TSR and can still call you even if you place your number on the registry. (These include long-distance phone companies, airlines, and insurance companies that operate under state regulations.) However, most telemarketing calls are placed by professional telemarketing companies, and they are not exempt—even if they are calling on behalf of an exempt company. The bottom line: professional telemarketers cannot call you if you are on the registry.

Certain other businesses are not required to go by the list. For example, an organization with which you have an established business relationship can call you for up to 18 months after your last purchase, payment, or delivery—even if your name is on the national "do not call" registry. And companies to which you've made an inquiry or submitted an application can call you for three months. However, if you ask a company not to call you it must honor your request, even if you have an established business relationship.

If you place your number on the national registry, you may give written permission to particular companies from whom you want to hear. And, if you don't put your number on the national registry, you can still prohibit individual telemarketers from calling by asking them to put you on their company's "do not call" list.

One more important point: although callers soliciting charitable contributions do not have to search the national registry, for-profit telemarketers calling on behalf of charitable organizations must honor your request to be put on their "do not call" lists.

How Does the National "Do Not Call" Registry Square with State Lists?

Many states have "do not call" registries. The FTC is working to coordinate the national "do not call" registry with these states to avoid duplication. This process will take a year or more; check the FTC's Web site or your state attorney general's office for details.

Unauthorized Billing

Before billing charges to your credit card account, telemarketers will be required to get your express informed consent to be charged a specific amount. If a telemarketer has your account information before the call and offers you goods or services on a free-trial basis before charging you automatically—also known as a "free-to-pay conversion" offer—the telemarketer must get your permission to use a particular account number; ask you to confirm the number by repeating the last four digits; and, for your protection, record the entire phone transaction.

Caller ID Transmission

Telemarketers will be required to transmit their telephone number and, if possible, their name to your caller ID service. This will protect your privacy, increase telemarketer accountability, and help law enforcement efforts. This provision will take effect one year after the release of the TSR.

The FTC enters Internet, telemarketing, identity theft, and other fraud-related complaints into Consumer Sentinel, a secure, online database available to hundreds of civil and criminal law enforcement agencies in the U.S. and abroad. To file a complaint or get information on consumer issues, visit http://www.ftc.gov or call toll-free 1-877-FTC-HELP (1-877-382-4357) or TTY 1-866-653-4261.

CHAPTER 6
Surveillance

Wherever You Go, There You Are!

➢ **Spyware**

➢ **I Spy**

I had a little dreidel. I made it out of clay. And when it's dry and ready, with my dreidel I will play.

—Children's Folk Song (Jewish)

When I switched on my computer last Tuesday, I was welcomed by the black screen of death, an error message that read, "Operating System Not Found." I don't know whether this has ever happened to you, but I'll tell you that it can make a grown man cry! Yes, I had an old backup, but I couldn't recall how recent. That's not a good sign. So for two long days and nights I worried about the state and fate of my data. Five completed chapters of this book, all of my diligent research, my Outlook address book with thousands of contacts, and every damn file on my 30-gig hard drive might be hosed into unrecoverable digital purgatory!

Fortunately, this story has a happy ending: I recovered my data. After two motherboard replacements by an onsite computer repair specialist, as well as three new hard drives, Dell upgraded my (un)trusty old laptop with a refurbished top-of-the-line model. Few companies stand behind their products like Dell or exhibit such integrity! I did lose a few weeks over the episode, but I got a much better laptop for my trouble.

After transferring all of my data to my new Dell Inspiron 8100 notebook and running Windows Update, the first thing I did was search for a utility that would mirror and back up my work in the event of another catastrophic computer crash. Ghostfiles, a freeware utility by lowrieWeb, wasn't hard to find. The program replicates any changes made to a file in one directory to a duplicate file in a second directory. Each character is mirrored by this nifty little app as I type. The final Part of this book, "Zone Defense," contains a section on backup strategies, including how to work with programs like Ghostfiles. You'll find a link to download Ghostfiles and other useful utilities on the Invasion of Privacy homepage at http://www.mjweber.com/iop/privacy.htm.

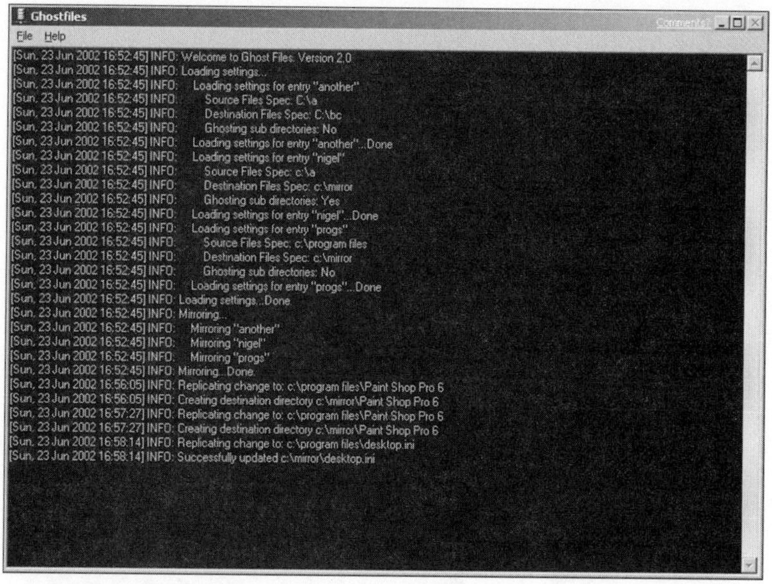

Ghostfiles

File   Help

```
[Sun, 23 Jun 2002 16:52:45] INFO: Welcome to Ghost Files. Version 2.0
[Sun, 23 Jun 2002 16:52:45] INFO: Loading settings.
[Sun, 23 Jun 2002 16:52:45] INFO:    Loading settings for entry "another"
[Sun, 23 Jun 2002 16:52:45] INFO:       Source Files Spec: C:\a
[Sun, 23 Jun 2002 16:52:45] INFO:       Destination Files Spec: C:\bc
[Sun, 23 Jun 2002 16:52:45] INFO:       Ghosting sub directories: No
[Sun, 23 Jun 2002 16:52:45] INFO:    Loading settings for entry "another"...Done
[Sun, 23 Jun 2002 16:52:45] INFO:    Loading settings for entry "nigel"
[Sun, 23 Jun 2002 16:52:45] INFO:       Source Files Spec: c:\a
[Sun, 23 Jun 2002 16:52:45] INFO:       Destination Files Spec: c:\mirror
[Sun, 23 Jun 2002 16:52:45] INFO:       Ghosting sub directories: Yes
[Sun, 23 Jun 2002 16:52:45] INFO:    Loading settings for entry "nigel"...Done
[Sun, 23 Jun 2002 16:52:45] INFO:    Loading settings for entry "progs"
[Sun, 23 Jun 2002 16:52:45] INFO:       Source Files Spec: c:\program files
[Sun, 23 Jun 2002 16:52:45] INFO:       Destination Files Spec: c:\mirror
[Sun, 23 Jun 2002 16:52:45] INFO:       Ghosting sub directories: No
[Sun, 23 Jun 2002 16:52:45] INFO:    Loading settings for entry "progs"...Done
[Sun, 23 Jun 2002 16:52:45] INFO: Loading settings...Done
[Sun, 23 Jun 2002 16:52:45] INFO: Mirroring...
[Sun, 23 Jun 2002 16:52:45] INFO:    Mirroring "another"
[Sun, 23 Jun 2002 16:52:45] INFO:    Mirroring "nigel"
[Sun, 23 Jun 2002 16:52:45] INFO:    Mirroring "progs"
[Sun, 23 Jun 2002 16:52:45] INFO: Mirroring...Done
[Sun, 23 Jun 2002 16:56:05] INFO: Replicating change to: c:\program files\Paint Shop Pro 6
[Sun, 23 Jun 2002 16:56:05] INFO: Creating destination directory c:\mirror\Paint Shop Pro 6
[Sun, 23 Jun 2002 16:57:27] INFO: Replicating change to: c:\program files\Paint Shop Pro 6
[Sun, 23 Jun 2002 16:57:27] INFO: Creating destination directory c:\mirror\Paint Shop Pro 6
[Sun, 23 Jun 2002 16:58:14] INFO: Replicating change to: c:\program files\desktop.ini
[Sun, 23 Jun 2002 16:58:14] INFO: Successfully updated c:\mirror\desktop.ini
```

Figure 6.1 *Ghostfiles window*

Spyware

Now think of Ghostfiles in a different context. Imagine if your every keystroke was mirrored without your knowledge and routed to somebody else's server. That's how a "keylogger," one variety of spyware, works. Spyware is technology installed clandestinely on a computer for the express purpose of surveillance. Who installs it? Nosy bosses, suspicious spouses, anxious parents, but more often than not, we unwittingly install it ourselves. Spyware, and its first cousin, adware, piggyback on many freely available programs on the Internet unbeknownst to the downloader. Once installed, adware traces a user's activities and reports them to a database network generally operated by a marketing company. Spyware reports the prey's activities back to who installed it in the first place. Spyware is the digital equivalent of trespassing on personal property, technology that can track you and commandeer your computer. Several software firms have developed applications to combat spyware, while others put their faith in pending legislation to ban it. In the meantime, spyware and adware are surreptitiously installed on the hard drives of millions of unsuspecting computer users! Spychecker.com (http://www.spychecker.com), a popular Web site, lists in its database more than a thousand programs that currently install spyware. The next time you think about downloading software, search Spychecker.com first. You'll find a

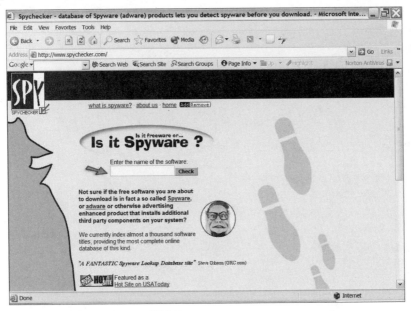

Figure 6.2 *Spychecker.com Web site*

link on the *Invasion of Privacy* homepage at http://www.mjweber.com/iop/privacy.htm

The Symptoms of Spyware

Your computer boots slower than usual and weird things happen with your Web browser. Suddenly, you're redirected to unfamiliar Web sites for no apparent reason. Your browser freezes, and Windows crashes! When you finally get to the bottom of it, if you ever do, you discover that some wacko has been tracking your every keystroke for weeks! It turns out your computer has been acting funny because a network of researchers has been hogging your CPU's clock-cycles to document the relationship between biorhythms and crop circles. This is known as *grid computing*, the utilization of CPU cycles from hundreds of individual computers networked to form a virtual supercomputer. To add insult to injury, when the smoke clears you learn your teenage son is totally to blame. Apparently, he inadvertently gave the grid network permission to use your computer for research when he downloaded a hot new game demo embedded with spyware! Grid computing is nothing new, but it's come back into vogue with the advent of broadband and multi-gigabyte CPUs. Gateway, the PC manufacturer, recently harnessed the power of 8,000 demo computers located throughout its 270 retail branches to form a new processor grid. Gateway claims their 8,000-computer grid can operate

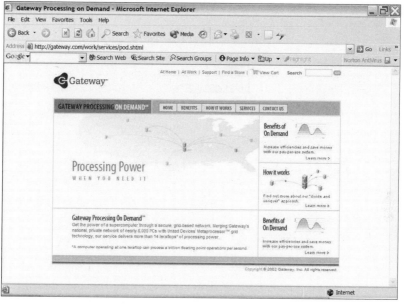

Figure 6.3 *Gateway Processing On Demand site*

at more than 14 TFLOPs (teraflops), processing power equivalent to that of the second fastest supercomputer on the planet. Gateway offers Processing On Demand for oil reservoir modeling, gene sequencing, pharmaceutical research, insurance risk assessment models, and crash test simulations. Whatever became of that nice spotted cow?

The Aureate/Radiate Go!Zilla Fiasco

The most rampant example of spyware I know of is Go!Zilla. Introduced a few years ago, Go!Zilla became the Internet's premier download manager. Millions of users downloaded it…that is, until word spread that the program installed secret DLLs (*Dynamic Link Libraries*) embedded by spyware giant Aureate/Radiate that tracked the surfing habits and download preferences of its users. Aureate—which later changed its name to Radiate because no one could pronounce it, or to remain elusive, or both—was installed on more than 30 million PCs worldwide, and it is still being installed with shocking regularity. More than 500 "advertising supported" programs currently install it. And it's nearly impossible to find Aureate/Radiate on the Internet unless you know where to look. A search on Google for "Aureate/Radiate" returns thousands of links to remove the spyware, but not one link to the company's Web site!

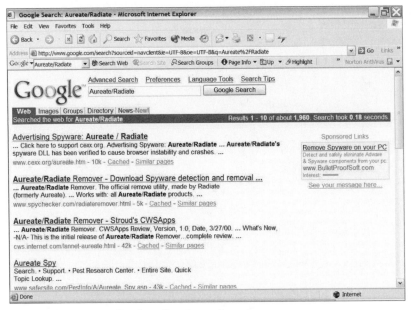

Figure 6.4 *Aureate/Radiate Google search results*

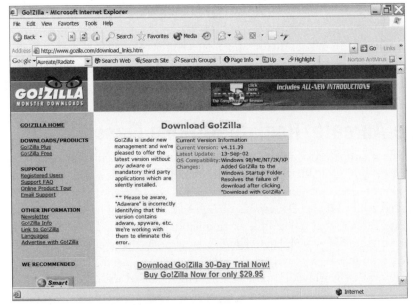

Figure 6.5 *Go!Zilla disclaimer*

Because of its tarnished reputation, Go!Zilla is under new management and claims version 4.11.39 is "free of any adware or mandatory third party applications which are silently installed."

However, buried within Go!Zilla's privacy policy is this little tidbit:

> **Traffic Analysis:** A software program is used to analyze traffic to this web site. This software does not create individual profiles for visitors. Unlike some tracking software, our software does not have a database of individual profiles for each visitor. Our software program collects only aggregate data.

As soon as I read this, I closed my Web browser and did a search for any new Aureate/Radiate components on my hard drive. If you want a download manager that doesn't contain spyware, I highly recommend SpeedBit's free Download Accelerator Plus, which has more than 50 million registered users.

A stable OS (*Operating System*) is a terrible thing to waste! Part II, "Zone Defense," includes detailed instructions on spyware removal and creating restore points in Windows XP and ME. Whenever I install new software, I always take these precautionary steps:

➤ Find out whether the program is listed in the Spychecker.com database.

➤ Create a Windows restore point before installing any new software.

➤ Scan any new program with antivirus software before launching.

➤ Scan the hard drive with Ad-aware or Spybot before launching.

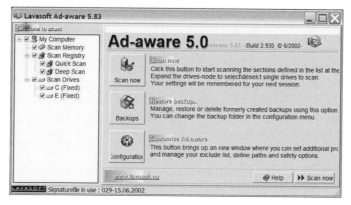

Figure 6.6 *Ad-aware screen*

I Spy

"Did you ever want to remotely monitor computers without having to physically access or install software?" That's the pitch for iSpyNOW.

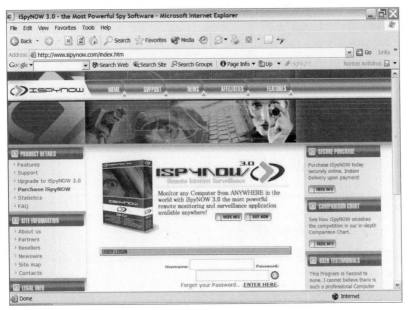

Figure 6.7   *iSpyNOW Web site*

iSpyNOW is a new breed of industrial-strength spyware that offers the ability to remotely install the software from any location in the world! "Simply send iSpyNOW as an e-mail attachment to the workstation or PP you wish to monitor remotely, and the program will install immediately! Once iSpyNOW has been installed, you have full control and monitoring power in real time of that remote PC! View chat conversations in real time, keystrokes, passwords, e-mail, remotely view the desktop and more! No one will know it is running; employees, children, not even your spouse!" That's a direct quote from iSpyNOW's old Web site. Mirko Zorz of Help Net Security (http://www.net-security.org) labels iSpyNOW a "serious breach of privacy" and considers the program a Trojan horse. For steps to prevent this kind of infection on you PC refer to Part II, "Zone Defense."

iSpyNOW surveillance features include

> **Internet Conversation Logging**. Log both sides of all chat conversations for AOL/ICQ/MSN/AIM Instant Messengers and view them in real time, as they are happening!

> **Window Activity Logging**. Capture information on every window with which you interact.

> **Application Activity Logging**. Track every application/executable with which you interact and execute.

> **Clipboard Activity Logging**. Capture every text and image item sent to the Clipboard on the remote computer.

> **Keystroke Monitoring**. Track all keystrokes (including hidden system keys) and the windows in which they were pressed. You can also pass keystrokes through a formatter for easy viewing and exporting.

> **Web Site Activity Logging**. Log all Web sites that you access on the remote computer.

> **System Control**. Instantly reboot or shut down the remote computer, or log off the current user.

This is one hell of a scary application! How much do you think a program like iSpyNOW costs? A thousand bucks, or at least a couple hundred? That's what I would have guessed. iSpyNOW costs

> $79 per license for 1–9 licenses

> $73.45 per license for 10–19 licenses

> $65.40 per license for 20–27 licenses

> $60.99 per license for 28–35 licenses

> $55.99 per license for more than 36 licenses

Its cheap price and ready availability make iSpyNOW easily available to anyone. It could be running on your computer right now whether you're a remote user or on a corporate network. Anyone who invests $79 can install it on your computer so be forewarned. That's the kind of world we live in! Both Mirko Zorz and George Kurtz (Foundstone) have pointed out to me that UNIX and Mac are less susceptible to spyware than Windows. While this is true to a point – there is far less spyware and adware for the UNIX platform—my research has uncovered spyware for both. Net Spy Software's Spector (http://www.netspysoftware.com/spectormac.html) is similar to iSpyNOW but runs on a Mac and UNIX keyloggers can be found at http://keystroke-loggers.staticusers.net/unix.shtml. The evils of technology can not be avoided! The best defense, indeed our only defense, is cognizance.

Workplace Surveillance

Is your employer using software like iSpyNOW to monitor you? According to a survey conducted by the Privacy Foundation, Nielsen/Net Ratings, the U.S. Bureau of Labor Statistics, and the International Labour Organization, 14 million employees—just over one-third of the online workforce in the United States—have their Internet or e-mail use under continuous surveillance at work. Worldwide, the number of employees under such surveillance is 27 million, just over one-quarter of the global online workforce. The online workforce is defined as "those employees who have Internet and/or e-mail access at work and use it regularly." A word to the wise: If you use your company's computer equipment and network, even off the premises, the odds are one-in-three that your employer is spying on you!

Minority Report

One look at Stanley Kubrick's masterpiece, *2001*, reveals how fallible we humans can be at predicting the future. There are no resorts on Jupiter or talking computers like HAL. Bill Gates still has a hard time keeping Windows from crashing (ditto for Steve Jobs and the Mac), and unfortunately there is no intergalactic travel. However, I recently saw Steven Spielberg's *Minority Report*, and its depiction of the future is dead on! Spielberg assembled a team of "futurists" beforehand to get the technology right. Among them were city planner Joel Garreau, anthropologist Steve Barnett, Neil Gershenfeld of the Media Lab, and Jaron Lanier, a composer and computer scientist best known for his work in virtual reality. The movie, based on a short story by Philip K. Dick, presented a parade of technology on the cusp of reality—biometric identification, presence awareness technology, an array of digital surveillance methodologies, and targeted personal advertising. But this technology has nothing to do with the future. It already exists!

Presence Awareness Technology

Presence awareness technology is a new killer app based on the theory that appliances on a network can automatically detect other appliances on that network. For example, placing a phone call has always been a shot in the dark because you don't know whether the person you're calling is there. Right? Now imagine knowing, without dialing that person's number, whether his phone is in use—or, if it's a cell phone, whether it's even on. That's the principle behind an emerging technology called *presence awareness*. In the near future, you'll be able to determine the whereabouts of any owner of a wired or wireless device, and vice versa! Other people will be able to determine where you are and figure out what you're doing.

According to Sonu Aggarwal, the CEO of Cordant, a company in Bellevue, Washington that develops instant-messaging technology

> The days of phone tag are over! This is a very powerful concept with long-term implications. In the future, presence awareness technology will be so integrated that a traveler could wear a wireless badge that interacts with a computer on the back of an airplane seat. When the computer senses the traveler is seated, it could automatically redirect messages to the computer's screen or send word to the traveler's contacts that he was onboard.

In the foreseeable future, presence awareness technology will be as ubiquitous as communication devices themselves! This year Motorola will roll out a new system that allows a caller to determine whether another person's mobile phone is on and in use. Nokia and Ericsson, among other telecommunications giants, are developing similar technology for wireless as well as landlines. Presence awareness technology is also being deployed on laptop computers and wireless PDAs, and in vehicle communications systems. The sky's the limit. New devices will be able to use GPS (*Global Positioning Systems*) to track the location of a person at any given moment!

Instant Messaging

Presence awareness technology has been around for a while in the guise of instant messaging programs. By tracking the activity of people on a buddy list, IM users can analyze login information to get a picture of people's routines—when they arrive at work, when they leave, how long they've been on or away from their computers, and when they're online at home. Employers, coworkers, friends, family, and even curious strangers can now analyze information that was once private (or at least hard to obtain) with little or no effort. "When you use these technologies you really expose yourself and your day to a lot of people," asserts Bonnie A. Nardi, an anthropologist at Agilent Technologies, a Palo Alto company that develops high-tech monitoring devices. After spending years studying instant messaging, Dr. Nardi became acutely aware of the subtle impact presence awareness technology has on people's lives. Nardi cautions, "It's time to think about what we want people to know about what we're doing at any given moment!"

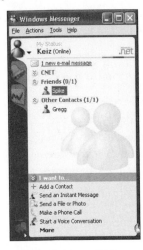

Figure 6.9A *MSN Instant Messenger*

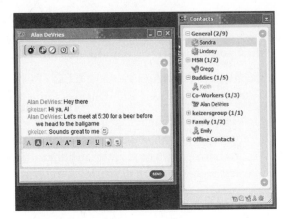

Figure 6.9B *Trillian Instant Messenger*

On the flip side, many people find it reassuring that presence awareness technology can monitor the remote activities of their inner circle, family, and friends. Meanwhile, the software industry is hard at work dreaming up ways to capitalize on this emerging technology. Dynamicsoft, a developer in New Jersey, is exploring how presence awareness software combined with wireless hand-held computers and GPS tracking could notify a person when a friend is in the immediate radius. As noted, the only example of presence awareness technology in use today is instant messaging, but if IM's popularity is any indication, people may be ready to embrace the broader implications of presence detection without much debate.

More than 50 million Americans currently use instant messaging products. Many report that their favorite feature is the ability to see whether their buddies are online. But even IM's strongest enthusiasts acknowledge some trepidation about remotely broadcasting their whereabouts. Cordant's Aggarwal uses MSN Messenger, which displays a clock icon in the contact list to indicate when a person has not touched the keyboard or mouse for a short period of time. As soon as the person resumes use of his keyboard or mouse, the clock goes away. Often Mr. Aggarwal gets a phone call the minute he hits his keyboard, and the caller is invariably someone who had been waiting for that icon to disappear. "Without my being aware, people are watching me!" Aggarwal admits.

Software developers maintain they can create presence awareness systems to accommodate both those who seek privacy and those who want contact.

image stabilization technology made the implementation of CCTV inevitable—even before the 9/11 attack made it a necessity, as many now argue.

Although the ACLU has no objection to cameras at specific, high-profile public places that are potential terrorist targets (such as the U.S. Capitol), the organization believes that the impulse to blanket our public spaces and streets with video surveillance is a bad idea. In Washington D.C., for example, the police are in the process of setting up a centralized surveillance center where officers can view video from schools, neighborhoods, Metro stations, and prominent buildings around the city. The use of sophisticated systems by police and other public security officials is particularly troubling in a democratic society, according to the ACLU. Here are the four primary reasons:

1. Video surveillance has not been proven effective.
2. CCTV is susceptible to abuse.
   - Criminal Abuse
   - Abuse for Personal Purposes
   - Discriminatory Targeting
   - Voyeurism
3. The lack of limits or controls on cameras use.
   - A consensus on limits for the capability of public CCTV systems
   - Legally enforceable rules for the operation of such systems
4. Video surveillance will have a chilling effect on public life.

Check out the ACLU archives at http://www.aclu.org/privacy/privacy.cfm? ID=12706&c=39 for more detail on each of these reasons.

Like any invasive technology, the benefits of deploying CCTV must be balanced against its costs and dangers. The bottom line for the ACLU is that the risks outweigh the benefits. They conclude CCTV has the potential to "change the core experience of going out in public because of the chilling effect surveillance will have on American citizens." They also conclude that CCTV "carries real dangers of abuse and 'mission creep,'" and that it "would not significantly protect America against terrorism."

The arguments for or against the deployment of CCTV are academic. CCTV is here regardless of public opinion! My concern is that Americans will exhibit the same blasé complacency toward CCTV displayed by our European counterparts. Here are the results from a recent newspaper poll held on Britain's Isle of Wight.

Yahoo! and Microsoft both include privacy features in their instant messa
ing products. Users must grant permission before their names can be add
to a person's contact list. But AOL Instant Messenger (both the stand-alo
version and the one embedded in AOL's Internet service) does not allow th
level of control. A user has no way of knowing whether someone has adde
his screen name to a buddy list! Whether people will use the built-in pe
mission blocking features raises another question. Many teenagers who u
instant messaging programs daily insist they won't block their friends becaus
they don't want to insult them. It appears peer pressure and etiquette ar
powerful disincentives when it comes to protecting one's own privacy.

The Internet Engineering Task Force, a group that develops standards fo
Internet communication, has been defining new standards for presenc
awareness and instant messaging technology. Dr. Jonathan Rosenberg, a coauthor of the task force and chief scientist for Dynamicsoft, believes he ha
come up with a solution to the social dilemma of managing one's privacy
without appearing rude. His idea is called "polite blocking," and it is based on
the same principle as using a digital doppelganger. Users appear to be busy or
off-line when in reality they're not, an alternative that keeps people guessing.
For example, a contact may determine your cell phone is on, but the phone
could be sitting on a table in your empty living room. Craig Peddie, a scientist working on presence awareness at Motorola, puts it this way: "Until we
get to the bio-implant stage, we won't really be able to determine whether
your cell phone is on you or not!"

Photo Surveillance

I bet you thought this chapter was going to be about nanny cams, lipstick
cams, and photo enforcement? It is, but first I want to stress that surveillance
often has nothing to do with a camera. With that
proviso, the Unites States is a laggard in the deployment of CCTV systems (closed-circuit television).
Americans have always prided themselves on the
right to privacy as defined under the Fourth
Amendment of the Constitution, which is the primary reason why the United States has been slower to
adopt CCTV than allies like Great Britain and
Canada. That's water under the bridge! CCTV is
already up and running in major metropolitan centers
such as Washington D.C. and New York City, and it
is coming to your neighborhood soon! Advances in

Figure 6.10

Photo enforcement

Q: Should we be concerned by the increasing use of CCTV in public places?

Results:

Yes (27.0%)

No (73.0%)

According to a recent study by Pew Research, 64 percent of American Web surfers have shared or are willing to share personal information to use a Web site. Sixty-eight percent report that they aren't worried that someone else knows what sites they visit. The greatest threat to our security and privacy is not from hackers, crackers, or Big Brother; it's from our own ignorance!

Image Stabilization Technology

When I started shooting commercials back in the seventies, image stabilization amounted to a crazy cameraman grasping a hand-held camera and hanging out of a helicopter by a bungee cord. Nowadays, police, military, and news choppers are outfitted with distinctive ball-shaped pods that house remote-control video cameras enhanced with image stabilization. Without image stabilization, there would have been no Rodney King, no L.A. riots, and no slow-speed freeway pursuit of O. J. Simpson. Image stabilization technology is the genie that let photo-reconnaissance out of the bottle.

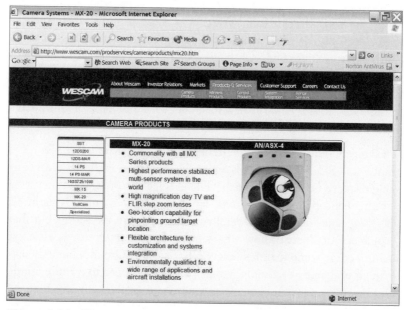

Figure 6.11 *Wescam aerial pod*

Therefore, it's only fitting that these events transpired near Hollywood, because Hollywood and the military-industrial complex codeveloped aerial surveillance.

The granddaddy of aerial surveillance is the Wescam—short for Westinghouse Camera—developed in the early 1960s by a Canadian subsidiary of Westinghouse as a battlefield surveillance tool for the Canadian military. Eliminating the vibration from the helicopter was the first step. The original Wescam ball was attached to a helicopter by shock absorbers that used springs and other motion damping devices. Simply eliminating vibrations didn't restrict three other types of camera movement—pitch (plunging up and down), yaw (rotating on a vertical axis), and roll (side-to-side rotation that creates a moving horizon). To deal with pitch, yaw, and roll, the inventors of the original Wescam used large gyroscopes to create inertia. Three gyros inside the camera ball are oriented to offset each of the three unwanted motions. Motors attached to the camera allow an operator inside the helicopter to view images on a video monitor and aim the camera as needed. The Wescam gyro stabilization system proved so steady that it has not significantly changed in more than three decades!

The Wescam system did have one significant drawback. Upkeep! It was prohibitively expensive to own because gyroscopes require routine maintenance. After a management-led buyout in 1987, the engineers who purchased Wescam devoted themselves to introducing image stabilization that was more robust, hence more affordable. Instead of providing stability, the three gyros in the second-generation Wescam wobble slightly when the rig changes directions. Sensors measure the wobbling and feed that data to microprocessors that use high-speed electric motors to move the camera and offset the unwanted motion. New systems built around electronic motion-sensing technologies are so stable that only the horizon and haze limit how far an observer can see. And the new technology is far more affordable; that's why police and news choppers have become so ubiquitous.

If the Orange County Sheriff's Department needs a car followed discreetly, Sergeant Frank Sheer can keep tabs on it from 3,000 feet in the air and a considerable distance behind the vehicle. The average motorist would never be aware that a helicopter is even around, let alone watching him. Flying in his chopper, Sergeant Sheer can be literally miles away from the action, but that does not mean he doesn't know what's going on. Sheer often has a clearer picture of a crime scene than his fellow officers on the ground. Nobody disputes the importance of technology that enables the police to capture criminals and rescue people, but some privacy advocates express concern that the recent proliferation of airborne cameras and their growing capabilities means that anyone who steps outside his front door could be the unwitting target of aerial surveillance.

"At 1,500 feet we can't read license plates yet," says Sergeant Sheer, "but we can tell if it's a man or a woman on the ground." Like many systems used by the police and the military, one of Orange County's two Wescam systems has a night-vision camera that creates images by capturing the infrared radiation emitted by warm objects, including people and marijuana grow houses! However, a ruling by the United States Supreme Court last June forced the Orange County Sheriff's Department and other police organizations to change the way they use thermal imaging photography. The Court ruled that the police "could not train thermal imaging cameras on private homes without a search warrant."

The legal skirmishes over surveillance and privacy have just begun! In the meantime, the technology continues to evolve. Four years ago Wescam introduced a third-generation image stabilization system that combines even greater stability with the reliability of cameras like those used by the Orange County Sheriff. It replaces spinning mechanical gyroscopes with fiber-optic gyros, which use bursts of laser light to calculate movements in each direction by the camera system. Not only is the new system much faster, it also provides a steady image within the magnification range of any manmade lens. The atmosphere and the impossibility of seeing beyond the horizon are the only factors that limit how far one can see. Wescam calls their new system a "ground-based Hubble telescope."

> We're all subject to surveillance! Cameras are watching us, and presence awareness technology, including spyware, is tracking our every movement.

If I made this statement 20 years ago, they would've locked me up in an asylum and thrown away the key. Today it's not even subject to debate. That's the problem: It should be! That's why I wrote this book.

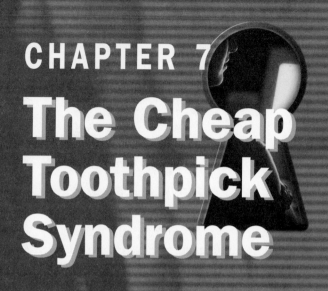

CHAPTER 7

The Cheap Toothpick Syndrome

Mediocrity and Hypocrisy

➣ **Social Insecurity**
➣ **Corporate Heinie-Think**

We're drowning in a sea of mediocrity
and hypocrisy is the water!

Last month I had the pleasure of dining at one of New York's finest five-star restaurants. I must remark that the meal and service were superb. I wish I could say the same about the toothpicks! Although it's considered uncouth in some circles, I like to pick my teeth after a good meal. I haven't exited a restaurant in the past 20 years without pinching a handful of toothpicks on my way out the door. I've got quite a collection, and I consider myself a toothpick connoisseur. It just so happens that this pricy establishment, which charged my party more than $90 a head, had the cheapest toothpicks I've ever come across! The wood was soft, the points were blunt, and they were wrapped in sticky cellophane. To make matters worse, they splintered the minute you stuck one in your mouth!

This got me wondering. Why would one of Manhattan's premier restaurants offer such crappy toothpicks in light of the fact that many inexpensive establishments offer toothpicks of superior quality? Toothpicks wrapped in starched white paper with sharp pointy ends and square middles, made of durable lumber—the toothpick equivalent of a Louisville Slugger! I did some research, which wasn't as easy as I imagined. The toothpick industry is very tightly knit and very tight-lipped. Finally, a sales rep from Danville Paper & Supply in Danville, Illinois, broke the code of silence.

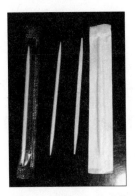

Figure 7.1 *Toothpick comparison photo*

Apparently it all boils down to economics. As you can see from Danville's Web site, the round-tip, square-middle wood Forster toothpick costs $1.39 per box, whereas the round economy hotel model sells for only $0.52 a box—a whopping 269 percent less. The reason this pricy restaurant offered its patrons such cheap toothpicks is because the person responsible for buying

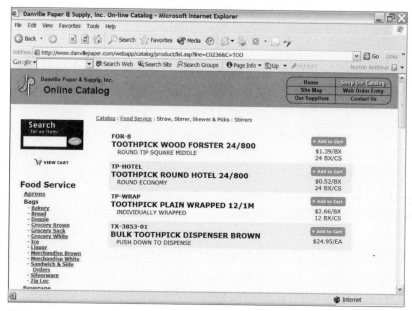

Figure 7.2 *Danville Supply online toothpick catalog*

the restaurant supplies economized on the toothpicks to save his establishment a few measly bucks! I wondered how much this clown could save every year by doing that, so I did the math.

> 500 toothpicks per night × 365 days a year = 182,500 toothpicks a year
>
> 182,500 toothpicks ÷ 800 toothpicks per box = 228 boxes of toothpicks a year

Wood Forster toothpicks

228 boxes × $1.39 = $316.92 a year

Economy Hotel toothpicks

228 boxes × $.52 = $118.56 a year

$316.92 (Wood Forster) − $118.56 (Economy Hotel) = $198.36 yearly savings

The bottom line is, to save a couple hundred bucks—one-tenth of a penny per toothpick—this world-famous restaurant offers its patrons inferior toothpicks. This book examines the mentality of mediocrity, which I call the "cheap toothpick syndrome," in upcoming chapters. Mediocrity has permeated every segment of our society and is at the root of America's problems.

Take the 2000 presidential election. What percent of the voting-age population cast a ballot? Here are the statistics from the U.S. Census Bureau.

Voting-Age Population	Registered Voters	Actual Turnout	Percent of Voting-Age Population	Percent of Registered Voters
209,128,094	159,725,715	105,411,587	50.41%	66.00%

One out of every two Americans eligible to vote didn't! Fewer than seven out of every ten Americans who bothered to register also didn't vote. What's their excuse? People who don't vote invariably cite two reasons.

> Their vote is meaningless because it won't affect the outcome.

> The mediocrity of the candidates compelled them to sit out this election.

Gore and Lieberman actually won the popular vote, so considering the actual outcome, the first argument doesn't hold water.

Presidential Ticket	Popular Vote	Percent of Popular Vote	Electoral Votes	Percent of Electoral Votes
Bush/Cheney (R)	50,459,624	47.87%	271	50.4%
Gore/Lieberman	51,003,238	48.38%	266	49.4%
Other	3,874,040	4%	–	–

Even the votes accumulated by third-party candidates such as Nader and Buchanan would have swung the election either way if a fraction had been cast for Bush or Gore. The second argument is even more specious. I believe the hypocrisy of those Americans who didn't vote, not the mediocrity of the candidates, is most responsible for the quality of our leaders (or lack thereof). Their excuse for not pulling the lever on Election Day is just another example of the cheap toothpick syndrome—the mentality of hypocrisy and mediocrity!

Social Insecurity

One of the most egregious examples of mediocrity I know of has to do with your Social Security number. Like me, I bet you have your number memorized because the first thing you're taught when you're a little kid is not to carry your Social Security number in your wallet. Well, I have bad news. The odds are that your Social Security number is in your wallet right now! Take your wallet out and see. If you have health insurance—which I hope you do—your Social Security number is probably printed on your health insurance card. It is, isn't it? And you didn't know it. Do you imagine for a second that insurance companies are unaware that this outmoded identification protocol, which dates back nearly 70 years, is a security risk to millions of customers? Cheap toothpicks come in many forms!

Figure 7.3 *Blue Cross card (with cheap toothpick)*

Corporate Heinie-Think

Sheep walk in a row by sniffing each other's heinies. The insurance industry is guilty of "heinie-think," and they aren't alone. Unfortunately, mediocrity is the norm in corporate America. We're drowning in a sea of mediocrity, and hypocrisy is the water! Without hypocrisy, mediocrity would not be an option because the flip side of hypocrisy is integrity, and the opposite of mediocrity is excellence.

You'll meet several people throughout this book on a mission to confront mediocrity and hypocrisy. Why don't you join them?

What should you do the next time you get offered a cheap toothpick? Complain to the maitre d'!

CHAPTER 8
The Metaphysics of Hacking

Don't Eat Yellow Snow

"A hacker shall do no harm."

—The Original Hacker Credo (circa 1970)

The most profound lesson I've learned about hacking is that the perception most people have about hackers is a stereotype. In this chapter I'm going to attempt to clear up that misperception without falling into the same trap. Hackers are people. As you know, no person is 100 percent evil or 100 percent angelic. Each individual has gray areas; quirks, personality traits, weaknesses, strengths, likes, dislikes, opinions, and feelings that are the sum of who she is. One thing all hackers have in common is, when it comes to the loves of their life, computers are near the top of the list. That is just about the only sweeping statement one can make about hackers. Aside from that, each hacker I know is unique.

Black T-shirts are a distant second love. A few paragraphs down you'll read that "black T-shirts are the de rigueur hacker uniform." This doesn't mean that all hackers wear T-shirts that are black. It's a fine line! In order to present you with a three-dimensional picture of hackers, I've created a graphic device called the "Hacker Pyramid." As you can see by the series of illustrations, there are three dimensions to hacking.

The Three Sides of the Hacker Pyramid

The biggest stereotype, the face of hacking most people see, is represented by the first illustration, the "Hacker Pyramid." A big gray area starts with white at the bottom and stretches to pitch black, pure evil, at the apex; cyber-terrorists! There is no gray area when it comes to cyber-terrorists like Vitek Boden, Richard Reed, and the mass spammers behind the Sobig.F virus. They are our enemy! The same applies to crackers, hackers who turn to crime. I include piratez who distribute warez (Chapter 11) in the same category as crackers. You'll learn more about all of these terms as you read on.

Figure 8.1 *The pyramids*

The big gray area at the bottom of the Hacker Pyramid is where and how hacker newbies incubate. They become hollow bunnies, script kiddies, and ankle biters before graduating to something else. The irony is that the people who are the hardest on hollow bunnies, script kiddies, and ankle biters, are hackers who've grown-up. I think they sometimes forget they were once newbies themselves.

A pyramid has three sides, but most people see only one of those sides. They're populated by hackers as well. Hackers who've matured. The hackers on the Security Pyramid are employed to counteract the cyber-terrorists, crackers, piratez, and virus writers who victimize us. The hackers on the "IT Pyramid" are paid to develop, maintain, and deliver the technology we consume.

But here's a real conundrum. These *company hackers* on the IT Pyramid develop the most invasive technology of all! Where do you think pop-up ads, spam, and spyware come from? Big Business! I put corporations that track us, harvest our personal information, and sell it for a profit in the same category as crackers! So as you can see, there are no patent answers when it comes to the subject of hackers.

Nolite edere flavam nivem means "don't eat yellow snow" in Latin. It also sums up the philosophy of hacking. I wish I could take credit, but I picked up the phrase from Dwain, a hacker who ends all of his e-mail with this witty signature. Hackers are among the wittiest people I know! I have not had the pleasure of meeting Dwain in person. Rather, I stumbled upon his e-mail monitoring a hacker user group a few years back.

```
Author: Dwain (---xxxx.link.net)

Date: 03-08-01 23:57

Hackers seem to be having a field day on Yahoo! chat. While most are
script kiddies, there are some serious attacks going on there. Have
seen monitor hacks, windows do some strange things, like minimized
windows disappearing completely, CD-ROM attacks, etc. All manner of
mischief going on, and Yahoo! seems unable to defend itself, much less
the poor people logged on. Perhaps Yahoo! deserves this attention, but
there are good folks getting their butts kicked with little protec-
tion. A few with decent hacking skills are attacking the attackers,
but that is a one-on-one approach, and not effective for people in
other rooms. Any help?

Dwain
nolite edere flavam nivem (don't eat yellow snow)
```

A few weeks later, Dwain hit pay dirt.

```
Author: Dwain (---xxxx.link.net)

Date: 03-25-01 06:16

I finally got a partial script these kiddies are using, as one sent
one that was unfinished. Any idea how to go about blocking these?
Script follows.

Dwain

nolite edere flavam nivem (don't eat yellow snow)
```

I'll spare you the boring details, but a computer script that started like this followed:

```
clear
echo echo " Windows Crasher Shell Script By TARZAN from ILLeGaL CreW Turkey"
echo "
echo " crashes or disconnects vulnerable win 98/nt/2000 boxes"
echo " usage : ./wincrash sourceip dstip"
```

It took Dwain, an anonymous hacker most likely in his teens, 17 days, but he tracked down the malicious code that exploited Yahoo! Chat's vulnerability and posted it so his fellow hackers could concoct a script to combat it. Dwain's words and actions epitomize white hat hacking. In my book Dwain is a hero. That's why I dedicated this book to him and countless others like him!

Some of you may be asking, but what about "TARZAN from ILLeGaL CreW Turkey," the cracker who created the Windows Crasher Shell Script, or the script kiddies who distributed it? Hacking is a game, and you can't have a game without two sides. In the hacking game, the good guys are called *white hats* and the bad guys are called *black hats*. Not very original, but it makes the point.

The real villain of the Dwain saga isn't TARZAN or the so-called script kiddies. It's Yahoo! Feel free to substitute MSN, AOL, or eBay, all of which have been cracked due to lax security. I'll address that later, but here's the moral of this story: If all it takes is a few dozen lines of code to crack the biggest portal on the Internet, we all better watch our behinds!

At the very least, be aware that nameless, faceless hackers are watching your behind in cyberspace! You'll never know how many times an anonymous hacker may have saved your butt!

The Sport of Hacking

Hackers love networking with each other almost as much as they love computer networks themselves! Each summer, in the sweltering heat of Las Vegas, young hackers of every description descend on DEFCON, a convention the hackers themselves consider the Super Bowl of hacking. The party is held at the Alexis Park Resort. You'll never see a more outlandish array of black T-shirts, the de rigueur hacker uniform. Anyone over voting age, like me for example, stands out like a sore thumb. The hackers, mostly males in their teens to early twenties, already know each other from DEFCONs past, hacker user groups or by reputation. They're not nerdy, shy types, either. They're outgoing, gregarious, and as Dwain's *nolite edere flavam nivem* indicates, hackers have an urbane wit all their own. I call it hacker rap and a few T-shirts from Jinx Hackwear (http://www.jinxhackwear.com/) illustrate it!

At DEFCON, you're nothing unless you have something to brag about. That's what these kids are here for—bragging rights! The highlight of each DEFCON (2003 was number 11) is a contest, a digital variation of Capture the Flag. DEFCON's organizers, elite hackers and security experts in their own right, fortify a Web server with the latest security and antihacking technology. Then the hackers, each of whom has a laptop, split up into teams and attempt to crack the secure server. The first team that cracks the DEFCON

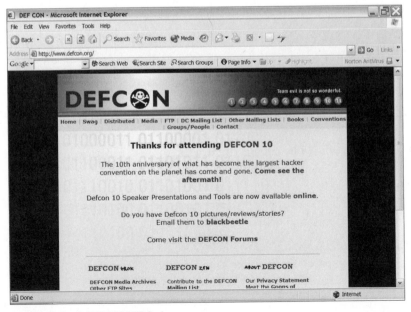

Figure 8.2 *DEFCON Web site*

server wins the contest, no small feat because most of these kids are extremely talented!

Winning the DEFCON challenge gives the winning team members more than mere bragging rights. It's a gold star on the resume of any budding-security expert. Winning the DEFCON challenge can help a winning member secure employment in computer security. Just like a high school jock dreams of a professional athletic career, high school hackers dream of becoming security experts when they grow up.

Before you can secure a computer network you must learn how to exploit and crack one. Before you can prevent computer viruses from spreading you must know how to write worms and viruses. That's the spirit behind DEFCON! The hackers come to learn and share what they know. There might not be a security slot for every hacker here, but there are occupational opportunities in technology for all those with hacking skills. Hacking is the minor leagues for every technology profession. The kids attending DEFCON today will be the architects of tomorrow's technology. As you can see from the DEFCON XI photo gallery, the pilgrimage is a hacker rite of passage.

The Business of Hacking

Some consider Jeff Moss, DEFCON's founder, the Tiger Woods of hackers. Moss is in his 30s, is married, and calls Seattle home. In addition to DEFCON, Moss created and moderates the Black Hat Briefings, a $1500-a-head security seminar attended by IT (information technology) professionals from the government and private sector. According to Moss

Figure 8.3 *Jeff Moss*

> The purpose of the Black Hat Briefings is to put the people developing the tools used by and against hackers face to face with the information managers who are being hacked. To accomplish this, we assemble a group of ven-
dor-neutral security professionals in the same room and let them talk candidly about the problems that networks face and the solutions to those problems. No frills, just straight talk by people who make it their business to explore the ever-changing security space. Spanning two days, topics include Intrusion Detection Systems

(IDS), Computer Forensics (CF), Incident Response, secure programming techniques, and tool selection for securing and effectively monitoring your network. The Black Hat Briefings also includes a separate track, nicknamed the White Hat Briefings, developed by the National Computer Security Center (NCSC) of the National Security Agency, specifically designed for CEOs and CIOs. While the Black Hat Briefings have a technology orientation, this track is intended for those who hire the organization's key security personnel.

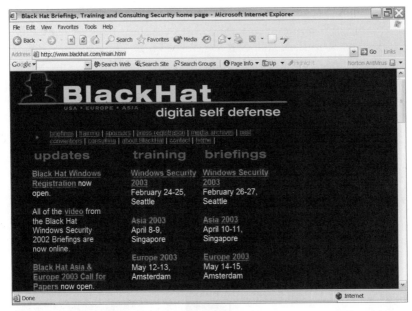

Figure 8.4 *BlackHat Web site*

The Hacker Pyramid

Almost every hacker I know claims they started hacking for two basic reasons.

1. **Curiosity.** They are curious and want to know how things work.
2. **The Rush.** That feeling you get from being somewhere you're not supposed to be.

Let's take a closer look at the hacker pyramid.

Figure 8.5 *The hacker pyramid*

Hollow Bunnies and Script Kiddies

As one rises from the bottom toward the top of the hacker pyramid, risk and illegality increase exponentially. The bottom of the pyramid is populated by hollow bunnies and script kiddies, curious newbies experimenting with the canned point-and-click hacking tools. Richard, a 28-year-old computer pro-

Figure 8.6 *Hacking Tools Web site*

grammer who has been hacking since age 11, calls the Web generation of hackers "hollow bunnies, like gigantic chocolate Easter bunnies filled with nothing but hot air!" Says Richard, "Ten years ago, hackers respected information as well as other people's personal property and computers. You had to possess knowledge and skills to hack! Nowadays, a novice who uses hacking software without any understanding of its function is much more likely to wreak havoc!"

Script kiddies are not generally malicious, but they can download buggy hacking tools that go awry or execute the wrong command and damage hundreds of computers or an entire network! Talk to any hacker over the age of 25, and he'll lament the passing of the good old days, when coding was an art form and learning how a computer system worked took patience, skill, and persistence.

Ankle Biters

Working our way up the hacker pyramid from the light into the gray shadows, you see the ankle biter. He possesses more hacking skills than his script kiddie cousin, and he crosses the line in terms of legality and danger. Canned denial-of-service attacks and paint-by-number Web site defacement are the ankle biter's forte. His intentions *are* malicious and may stem from boredom, curiosity, alienation, or anger. Although his motivation isn't necessarily criminal, his actions produce material and financial harm. Some ankle biters claim they're the Robin Hoods of cyberspace, righting a mighty wrong by creating graffiti on an offending Web site or bringing it to its knees with a denial-of-service attack. This behavior is diametrically opposed to the Original Hacker Credo, which dates back to the 1970s:

> A hacker shall do no harm.

The real Robin Hoods of cyberspace are the white hat hackers like Dwain, whom you met at the beginning of this chapter.

Ankle biters have three options:

➤ Evolve into a white hat

➤ Get busted

➤ Move up the hacker pyramid to become a cracker

Crackers

Crackers are the wise guys of cyberspace, skilled hackers who have crossed the line into criminality. Crackers work on their own or in teams, and sometimes they contract their services to organized crime, like digital hit men. Crackers are pure black hats who reside on the black side of the hacker pyramid.

Crackers come in two varieties—master criminals and small-time cons. The small fries perpetrate petty scams like auction frauds on eBay. They hit and run—if they're successful. Some victims turn the tables on these lowlifes! Eric Smith, a 21-year-old college student at the University of New Orleans, was swindled out of a brand new Macintosh PowerBook G4 on eBay last Christmas. Smith got so outraged that he tracked down his swindler, a con man living in Chicago. Smith set up his own sting and lured the con man into bidding on another computer. The con man took the bait and got an early visit from Santa Claus—cops from the Markham, Illinois, Sheriff's Department, who gave him a one-way sleigh ride to jail. Eric Smith got his revenge, but did he ever get his PowerBook back? You'll have to wait until Chapter 11 to find out.

Some crackers are legendary criminals, like the Russian gang that siphoned $10 million from Citibank without their knowledge, or the Amsterdam Mafia chief who had crackers access the police department computer so he could keep one step ahead of the law. Jeff Moss of DEFCON and the Black Hat Briefings says, "Crime syndicates approached hackers several years ago to work for them, but with so many easy-to-use hacking tools available today, criminals hardly need hackers to do their dirty work!"

Kevin Mitnick's New Leaf

Kevin David Mitnick is arguably the most famous American cracker. He was busted for hacking several times in the 80s while still a teenager. His rap sheet boasts some impressive cracks:

   Pacific Bell's COSMOS phone center in Los Angeles

   University of Southern California, where he was discovered sitting at a computer terminal breaking into the Pentagon over the ARPANET

   Digital Equipment's Palo Alto research laboratory

   The Santa Cruz Operation, a California software company

   California Department of Motor Vehicles

   Sprint

   TRW's credit reference computer

Mitnick went on the lam, eluding the FBI and cracking his way across America. But on Christmas Day, 1995, he made a fatal mistake. Mitnick hacked into the home computer of one of the world's most respected security experts, Tsutomu Shimomura, and then had the audacity to rub the crack in Shimomura's face. Shimomura tracked Mitnick down like a digital bounty hunter, first on the Internet and then to the closest cell phone transponder, resulting in Mitnick's arrest and incarceration. Their game of cat-and-mouse is the stuff of hacker legends and the subject of at least two books—*The Fugitive Game: Online with Kevin Mitnick* (Little Brown & Co, 1997), by Jonathon Littman, and *Takedown: The Pursuit and Capture of Kevin Mitnick, America's Most Wanted Computer Outlaw—By the Man Who Did It* (Hyperion, 1996), coauthored by John Markoff and Shimomura.

Figure 8.7 *Kevin Mitnick arrest photo*

Mitnick served five years in prison before being released on probation in 2000. One stipulation of his release was that Kevin was forbidden to touch a computer for the next three years.

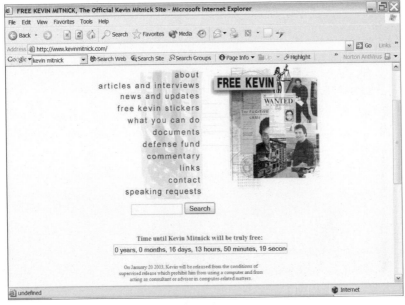

Figure 8.8 *Free Kevin Mitnick Web site*

Kevin Mitnick's Release Conditions

The Ninth Circuit issued the release conditions in a three-page written opinion.

The conditions of Mitnick's release, as they appeared in *United States v. Kevin David Mitnick*, CR 96-881-MRP, before the United States District Court for the Central District of California can be found at http://www.techtv.com/cybercrime/features/jump/0,23009,2110090,00.html.

He was not allowed to own, use, or touch a computer. He wasn't allowed to act as a consultant to anyone who did, or to own or use any altered telephone or wireless communication device.

Talk about the punishment fitting the crime! The most infamous hacker in American history wasn't able to lay a finger on a computer keyboard for almost eight years. On January 20, 2003, Mitnick was released from the conditions of supervised release, which prohibited him from using a computer and from acting as a consultant or advisor in computer-related matters. That day I watched Kevin log on to his girlfriend's website on Tech TV's "The Screensavers." The last time he touched a computer, it was a 486. Now he was surfing the Web on a Pentium 4. What a time warp! I was touched watching it. Kevin claims he turned over a new leaf, and I tend to believe him. He has a heck of a future as a security consultant and speaker, and Mitnick recently wrote a thought-provoking book entitled *The Art of Deception: Controlling the Human Element of Security* (John Wiley & Sons, 2002).

Figure 8.8 *The reformed Kevin Mitnick (left) and Sean "Jinx" Gailey (right) at DEFCON XI (courtesy Jinx Hackwear)*

DEFCON XI Photo Gallery

Sean "Jinx" Gailey (left) and Queue (drinking beer in b.g.) of Jinx Hackwear (courtesy Jinx Hackwear)

Jinx Hackwear booth (courtesy Jinx Hackwear)

Kevin Mitnick Wins Hacker's Jeopardy (courtesy Epiphany Port7alliance)

Hackers love networking (courtesy Epiphany Port7alliance)

Hacker chicks draw a crowd (courtesy Epiphany Port7alliance)

Hacker chicks boogie (courtesy Epiphany Port7alliance)

Epiphany (right) and Agent5 (left) of Port7alliance (courtesy Epiphany Port7alliance)

Jove was among the few restrained hackers at DEFCON (courtesy Epiphany Port7alliance)

Hacker Rap

Hacker Art

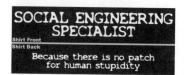

A look inside my head (by Epiphany Port7alliance)

eBay's Evil Twin—The Black Hat Cracker Auctions

Stolen creditcard numbers by the tens of thousands are sold on the Web every week, in a handful of membership-only Internet auctions that are a cross between eBay and the stock market. These auctions, in which credit-card prices fluctuate with supply and demand, cost financial institutions billions of dollars each year and indicate how readily personal information is stolen and traded. I didn't attend, but I have it on good authority—*The New York Times*—that an identity-theft convention for stolen creditcard resellers was held in Odessa, Ukraine, in late July 2001. According to one security expert who surreptitiously monitors the Internet creditcard market

> It's straight out of Capitalism 101. There are even Web banner ads. The market price of credit cards fluctuates daily based on supply, which is copious. There appears to be an endless supply of stolen credit cards out there! In recent days, the cost of a single credit card has ranged between 40 cents to five dollars, depending on the level of authenticating information provided. But the credit-card numbers are typically offered in bulk, costing $100 for 250 cards to $1,000 for 5,000 cards, for example, with the sellers offering guarantees that the creditcard numbers are valid.

Security experts say the buyers of stolen card numbers hail from all over the world, but the hot spots are the former Soviet Union, Eastern Europe, and Asia (specifically Malaysia). The buyers use the credit card numbers in a variety of fraudulent activities, including making purchases over the Internet, fencing them in the West, or even extracting cash advances directly from the creditcard accounts. Experts say residents of the former Soviet Union, often in Russia and Ukraine, operate the marketplaces and typically buy the card numbers from black-hat hackers. The crackers obtain the card numbers by breaking into the computer systems of online merchants and getting access to thousands of creditcard records at a time. According to Richard Power, editorial director of the Computer Security Institute, an association of computer security professionals that recently published a report with the Federal Bureau of Investigation on computer crime, "In the old days people robbed stagecoaches and armored trucks. Now they're knocking off servers!"

Registered users in the creditcard auctions generally number around 2,000. Operators frequently change their Web site addresses to avoid detection by law enforcement, but security professionals surreptitiously monitor the auctions anyway. That doesn't mean the bidders are easily caught because they don't use real names or reveal their whereabouts. Payments are made by secure wire transfers through Web sites like http://www.webmoney.ru in

Russia. The electronic deposits are then transferred into overseas bank accounts that are extremely difficult to trace. If this whole setup reminds you a bit of eBay or PayPal, it's because they were the original model. There's even a feedback forum, which proves once and for all that there is honor among thieves!

A 19-year-old dealer from Odessa, Ukraine, known as "Script," is considered among the most reliable of the stolen creditcard auctioneers. Here's one of his typical listings: "I'm selling Visa and MC (American cards). The minimal deal size is $40." He also listed a higher price if the deal included the card's CVV2 code, a printed security code that appears on credit cards and is supposed to prevent fraud. Merchants are not supposed to record the code in their databases, but they sometimes do, which means that crackers can get access to this higher level of information.

On the online forum, Script noted that 100 cards with CVV2 codes cost $300. A discussion involving his former buyers then ensued, attesting to his reliability. One buyer wrote, "This guy's always slightly more expensive, but his stuff is good." Another wrote, "This guy is awesome! He always gave me three times the number of cards I paid for." The endorsements are a surrealistic imitation of feedback forums on legitimate sites such as eBay and Amazon. Imitation is the sincerest form of flattery!

Cyber Terrorists

In April 2001, shortly after the collision between a U.S. spy plane and a Chinese jet fighter that crashed into the South China Sea, killing the Chinese pilot, an all out cyber war erupted between Chinese and American hackers. Following 11 tense days during which China held the 24-member crew of the U.S. surveillance plane in detention, U.S. crackers hacked hundreds of Chinese Web sites, leaving messages like, "We will hate China forever and hack its sites."

In response, the Honker Union (Chinese for *Red Hackers*) launched its own electronic graffiti blitz. One Chinese message read, "Don't sell weapons to Taiwan, which is a province of China." A U.S. hacker named pr0phet responded, "I want President Bush to know he is supported in his decision to support Taiwan by almost all the hackers I know." Companies on both sides of the Pacific scrambled to patch security holes. By the time a truce was declared, thousands of Web sites were defaced, which cost millions of dollars to repair.

The top rung of the hacker pyramid is reserved for cyber terrorists. Here's a sobering thought. Each December research giant IDC presents an annual forecast of major technology developments it anticipates in the upcoming year. IDC predicted "a major cyber-terrorism event will disrupt the economy and bring the Internet to its knees for a day or two in 2003. The event could take the form of a denial-of-service attack, a network intrusion, or even a physical attack on key network assets." Only eight months into 2003, IDC's forecast was on the nose! A triple whammy consisting of Sobig.F, the worst mass-mailing computer virus in history, the MSBlast worm (that targets Windows), and Nachi, the so-called "fixer worm" aimed at repairing damage caused by MSBlast, brought the Web to its knees that August. IDC missed the mark on one minor (not so minor) point. The triple whammy brought the Internet to its knees not for a day or two, but for weeks! It caused irreparable damage to countless personal computers. Not only were the financial losses incalculable, as fate would have it, the triple whammy occurred right on the heels of the power grid failure. Make no mistake about it. Cyber terrorism is here! And it has been for a while.

According to a story written by Barton Gellman for the *Washington Post* in the fall of 2001, just before 9/11, Detective Chris Hsiung of the Mountain View, California police department began investigating a suspicious pattern of surveillance of computer systems in Silicon Valley. Hackers from the Middle East and Southern Asia were exploring the networks used to manage Bay Area utilities and government offices. Hsiung, a specialist in high-tech crime, alerted the FBI's San Francisco computer intrusion squad.

Working with experts at the Lawrence Livermore National Laboratory, the FBI uncovered a trail of much wider digital reconnaissance. A forensic summary of the investigation, prepared by the Defense Department, said the Bureau found "multiple stakeouts of sites nationwide routed through telecommunications switches in Saudi Arabia, Indonesia, and Pakistan." The intrusions included emergency telephone systems, electrical generation and transmission, water storage and distribution, nuclear power plants, and gas facilities. According to Gellman's article, U.S. officials said some probes suggested planning for a conventional attack, while others homed in on digital devices that allow remote control of services such as fire dispatch and equipment pipelines. More information about these devices—and how to program them—turned up on Al Qaeda computers seized in 2002, according to law enforcement and national security sources. Did the government overlook yet another piece of the jigsaw puzzle that led to 9/11? Unsettling signs of Al Qaeda's skills in cyberspace have led some security experts to conclude that terrorists are at the threshold of using the Internet as a direct instrument for bloodshed!

The Stench Of Cyber Terrorism

Our air traffic control system, banking, Wall Street, and much more are vulnerable to cyber attack. You don't have to be a member of Al Qaeda to be a cyber terrorist, either. You can have financial motivations like the terrorists in the movie *Die Hard*. Gellman's *Post* article details a "for-profit" cyber-terrorism plot that's becoming urban legend.

On April 23, 2000, the police stopped a car on the road to Deception Bay in Queensland, Australia. Inside, they discovered a stolen computer and radio transmitter in the possession of the driver, one Vitek Boden. Using commercially available technology, Boden had turned his vehicle into a pirate command center for the entire sewage treatment system spanning Australia's Sunshine Coast. His arrest solved a mystery that had plagued the Maroochy Shire wastewater system for months. Hundreds of thousands of gallons of putrid sludge had leaked into parks, rivers, and the manicured grounds of a Hyatt Regency hotel. Marine life died, the creek water turned black, and the stench was unbearable! The red-faced managers at the sewage treatment facility had no explanation and no control. They were powerless, helpless, and clueless, until the day of Boden's capture!

The Boden case is cited as one of the few documented cases of *cyber terrorism*, the use of digital controls to damage a physical infrastructure. Security experts around the world have scrutinized it. It turns out Boden had recently quit his job at Hunter Watertech, the supplier of Maroochy Shire's remote control and telemetry equipment. Evidence at his trial suggests Boden was angling for a consulting contract to solve the very problem he caused! This is a tried and true hacker technique. How did he do it? The software on Boden's laptop identified itself as Pumping Station 4, and then suppressed all of the internal system alarms. Boden was the central control system during his intrusions, with unlimited command of 300 SCADA (*Supervisory Control And Data Acquisition*) nodes governing both sewage and drinking water. Like thousands of other utilities worldwide, Maroochy Shire allows its technicians to remotely operate the facility via digital controls. As an insider, Boden knew how the system worked and the software he used conformed to international standards. Of course, detailed manuals with step-by-step instructions on how to operate SCADA nodes by remote control are also available on the Internet.

Identical SCADA nodes run oil, gas, manufacturing, power, dams, and assorted American utilities. But perhaps the most vulnerable target is the North American power grid, described by Massoud Amin, a mathematician and security consultant, as *"the most complex machine ever built!"* Electricity has no substitute. Every other infrastructure depends on it. At a security conference hosted by the Commerce Department in April 2002, government and industry scientists agreed they have no idea how the North American power grid would stand up to a cyber attack. What they do know is that white hat mock intrusion teams from the Energy Department's four national labs have devised "eight scenarios for SCADA attack on an electrical power grid." All of them worked! To date, 18 such exercises have been conducted against large regional utilities. Prior to his resignation in 2002, Richard A. Clarke, the Bush Administration's cyber-security advisor, stated bluntly that, "the intruders have always succeeded." U.S. analysts believe that by taking command of an electrical power substation or the floodgates of a reservoir, cyber terrorists could use virtual tools to destroy lives and property in concert with "kinetic weapons" such as explosives. According to Ronald Dick, director of the FBI's National Infrastructure Protection Center, "The event I fear most is a physical attack in conjunction with a successful cyber attack on the responders' 911 system or the power grid!"

Where Were You When The Lights Went Out?

On August 14, 2003 a cascading power grid failure knocked more than 100 power plants, including 22 nuclear reactors, offline. The blackout blanketed 50 million people spanning a 9,300-square-mile radius that stretched from Canada to New England. The lights went out in all five boroughs of New York City and 80 percent of New York State. A million people in New Jersey, 1.4 million Ohioans, 2.4 million customers in Michigan, and tens of millions of Canadians were also in the dark. The chauvinistic cable news networks made Manhattan the epicenter of the story, perhaps because they all have street-level broadcast studios there. I'm certain that victims from Rochester, Cleveland, and Detroit would be appalled by the sort shrift they received if only they could have watched the reportage.

After the restoration of power, President Bush swaggered up to a microphone on his ranch down in Crawford, Texas and called the power grid failure "a wake-up call." Unfortunately, it takes a calamity to wake up most politicians! Bush apparently didn't heed Richard Clarke, his cyber-security advisor, when Clarke expressed public concerns about the vulnerability of the North American power grid in 2002, 16 months prior to the blackout.

There is still no definitive consensus on why the lights went out that day. After all is said and done, I'll be surprised if it isn't computer related. I'm not inferring it was malicious. It might've been a computer glitch.

Just because it wasn't cyber terrorism doesn't mean it couldn't have been! That's the conclusion most security experts have already drawn from the "Blackout of '03." It was the best "dry run" cyber terrorists could have gotten. If they planned it themselves, they couldn't have planned it better!

The Other Side of the Hacker Pyramid

The hacker pyramid reminds me of an old joke that revolves around a pack of Camel cigarettes. You display the front of the pack and ask: "If you were stranded in the hot sands of an arid desert in dire need of food, shelter, and water for your thirsty camel, what would you do?"

Before delivering the punch line, you turn the pack of Camels around and reveal the Casbah pictured on the reverse side. Then you answer, "I'd go around the corner and check me and my camel into the Casbah!"

Figure 8.10 *Front of a Camel cigarette pack*

A pyramid has three sides! The face of hacking most people see is the one described in Figure 8.5. Hollow bunnies and script kiddies are inexperienced newbies whose curiosity combined with powerful "point-and-click" hacking tools could inadvertently or purposely lead to damage or harm. Ankle biters are black hats, although many of them would argue their motivation is the same as white hats—to expose network security flaws. Crackers are black hats, cyberspace equivalents of a criminal underground. And cyber terrorists are the blackest cracker of all! However, for every

Figure 8.11 *Rear of a Camel cigarette pack*

black hat there is a white hat out to foil him with technology from the same bag of tricks. The story of hacking is an allegory of good versus evil!

Few people bother to walk around to see what's on the remaining two sides of the hacker pyramid. So let's turn the metaphoric pack of Camels around.

Figure 8.12 *The security pyramid*

Directly behind the hacker pyramid is the security pyramid. Everyone on this side of the pyramid (or on the third side—the IT pyramid—for that matter) is a hacker with proven skills.

White Hat Hackers

White hat hackers are the self-appointed vigilantes of cyberspace. They reside on the first rung of the security pyramid, and they hack for pleasure as well as justice. Dwain (*don't eat yellow snow*), whose story begins this chapter, typifies a white hat hacker. Righting the wrong of a mischievous script kiddie is a typical white hat mission. Many white hats, still in their teens, use their hacking skills as a calling card for future employment. Optyx, a hacker once interviewed by PC World magazine, got his first job while on a white hat mission when he was just 15. He'd been exploiting a security hole in a small ISP for months. Finally, he sent the administrator a note advising him to fix it. The administrator wrote back saying he didn't know how. Optyx sent him the code to patch the hole, and the administrator offered him a job. Now a 21-year-old security consultant, Optyx complains, "Fixing security holes is a thankless task. Most companies just focus on the fact that you hacked them and they want to come after you with a lawsuit. It's made hackers reluctant to help! Now I still fix machines, but I won't tell an administrator I've done it." Spoken like a true white hat!

Full Disclosure Advocates

Full disclosure advocates are the whistleblowers of cyberspace—hackers who believe information (especially information pertaining to security, freedom, and privacy) should be freely available. Full disclosure advocates counterbalance the status quo. Without them, the powers-that-be would have no accountability. The debate over the dissemination of information has raged between technology vendors and full disclosure advocates since the advent of computing. Thejian, a hacker historian, explains the debate over "full disclosure" versus "security through obscurity" this way:

> Nowadays, hackers are often portrayed as anything on two legs near something electric with the ability to break it! You may smash the stack for fun, profit, or just because you're a vicious little bugger, but the idea most hackers have about hacking is someone who opens stuff up just to find out how and why it works. The security scene consists of lots of people with different takes on how to act. At the crux of the debate is the issue of "full disclosure" versus "security through obscurity." These two philosophies are at loggerheads. Full disclosure advocates releasing all available information about security problems to the public in order to inform users how to prevent it from affecting their systems. The security through obscurity school maintains that information about security problems should be shared only among a select group of people. This places users at the mercy of vendors slow to produce a fix, and has resulted in an alarming number of security incidents that could have been prevented.
>
> Full disclosure does have a dark side. When something can be abused, it will be. That's human nature. Unfortunately, detailed information on how to exploit security problems appeals to a new breed of lazy hackers looking to save themselves the trouble of actually learning how to hack. When plug-and-play hacking tools were introduced, these script kiddies exploited them for nefarious purposes. The security through obscurity school contends that what you don't know can't hurt you. They compare full disclosure to giving a kid a gun. The full disclosure camp counters that it's worse when a kid finds the gun by himself. By teaching him how to use it, you can prevent him from shooting himself!

Big Network/Small World

More essays by Thejian, and other experts on hacking and security, are archived on Help Net Security at http://www.net-security.org/articles_main.php. This web site is an excellent example of disclosure advocacy. I relied on it for research as you can see. What you can't see is the impact Help Net Security had on this book.

I contacted the site and got to know the people behind it, a team of white hats who operate Help Net Security from their home base in Croatia. One thing led to another and, to make a long story short, Mirko Zorz and Berislav Kucan became the tech editors on this book. Their imprint is on every page. I not only relied on their hacking and security expertise, but they helped sensitize me to the sensibilities of hackers.

Figure 8.13 *Mirko Zorz and Berislav Kucan of Help Net Security*

Mirko and Berislav were born in Rijeka, Croatia, and both are in their 20s. Kucan started Help Net Security (www.net-security.org) in 1998, and Zorz joined him at the beginning of 2000. Help Net Security has been a leading source of information regarding the security scene for several years now. Help Net Security always tends to position itself as a source of guidance on how to approach security related issues in personal as well as business environments.

The Internet is a big network, but when it comes to hackers, it's a small world. The more hackers I got to know, the more apparent it became to me that most of them know each other, by reputation at the very least! It's almost as if the Internet is the hackers' own private club, invisible to the uninitiated. I want to thank Mirko, Berislav, Thejian, Dwain, Jinx, Epiphany, Jeff Moss, and all the other hackers who invited me in and treated me as a welcome guest.

instances of attempted corporate hacking in 2000—more than twice the number documented in 1999, and eight times the amount documented in 1995. In 2001, 52,658 incidents were reported—double the number of the previous year. Keep in mind that these are just reported incidents. To avoid negative publicity, most corporations have a "do not report" policy when it comes to being hacked. Security through obscurity strikes again!

In an ironic twist of fate, CERT, *the* "official" Department of Defense computer security clearinghouse (http://www.cert.mil/), was itself hacked by a denial-of-service attack in late May 2001. The most sophisticated hackers on the planet couldn't protect their own network, a security breach analogous to thieves burglarizing a police station!

Security Experts

In the parlance of the security business, a network intrusion is called an *incident*, and nullification of the breach is called a *response*. Security firms providing incident response have become one hot sector in technology. Gartner Research reports that businesses dedicated an average 0.4 percent of their annual revenue to security in 2001, a figure expected to increase tenfold by 2011, when security expenditures will account for 4 percent of a company's total annual revenue.

Security experts are the pop stars of the technology sector. George Kurtz of Foundstone, Jeff Moss of the Black Hat Briefings, and George Guninski of George Guninski Security Research spring to mind, but corporate giants like IBM and Symantec are also major vendors of security services. Actually, Peter Norton, of Norton Antivirus fame, was the original security superstar! The company he founded turned into Symantec. Last year Symantec's managed security division, which has operations centers in Texas and the United Kingdom, produced nearly $1 billion in revenue for fiscal year 2002. Symantec's security clients include 98 of the Fortune 100.

Security is hot because the Internet has come of age. The Internet links more than 20 million computers in 200 countries, and anything attached to the Internet is potentially hackable! Private networks are slightly more secure, but in this economy there's a need to pinch pennies and modernize. Those who still operate private networks realize that the Internet is less expensive and more efficient—if it can be trusted. That "if" is what security experts provide. Networks are vulnerable because there's no way to quantify their actual security; that's the conundrum. According to security expert George Kurtz, "The problem is there is no one system that allows you to qualify exposure to differentiate between how exposed one company is compared to another."

Foundstone, the security company that Kurtz co-founded, developed a 100-point scale for rating a company's exposure to unauthorized access, with 100 being the most secure. Kurtz says, "In general, any enterprise system is hard-pressed to get above 70 or 75. We just finished a large enterprise that got a 5. When we went through the process, we found many of their servers were already hacked!"

What are the crackers looking for? According to Kurtz, "We see some hackers who are looking to target specific organizations. They're looking to get source code. There is a lot of source code that floats around the Internet because organizations have been compromised. They're also looking to use those organizations as a staging point to launch other attacks, or they're looking to embarrass the organization. Then there are people who are just fishing. They're kind of throwing the hook out there and automatically scanning. And when they find something, they take advantage of it just because it's there!"

Most security experts have a subspecialty, such as network engineering, software development, system design, computer forensics, monitoring, attack and penetration detection, incident response, or digital surveillance. For that reason, and to maximize efficiency, most security consultants work in teams, and most security teams cooperate with each other. Figure 8.13 shows a graphic from Foundstone's Professional Services that illustrates how a security team functions—a closed circle of prevention, resolution, and response. For a more in-depth perspective on computer crime investigation, I highly recommend *Incident Response* (McGraw-Hill Osborne Media, 2001), the definitive book on the subject, written by Chris Prosise, a co-founder of Foundstone and Kurtz's partner.

Top Secret?

Richard Reed, the Al Qaeda shoe bomber, received all of his orders from anonymous computer terminals in Internet cafes scattered around the world. As luck would have it, he was too cheap to buy a Bic lighter, but he certainly knew how to use computers and surf the Web! That tells you something about our enemy. The Department of Defense admits its networks are probed around 250,000 times annually. It's impossible to tell whether these intrusions are from enemies out to steal our military secrets or hackers on a war-dialing joyride. Regardless, each probe is viewed as a potential threat.

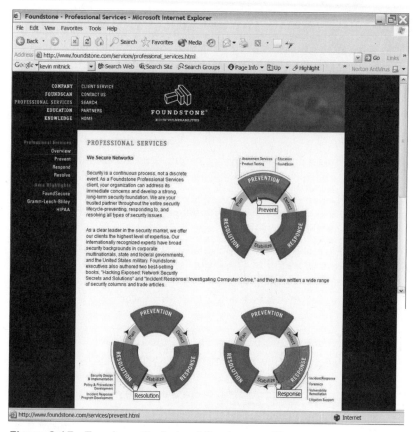

Figure 8.15 *Foundstone Professional Services page illustration*

According to Frank Cilluffo, Director of the Information Assurance task force at the Center for Strategic and International Studies (CSIS) in the nation's capital, "The likelihood of obtaining top secret information in this way is small since classified data is generally stored on machines not connected to the Net. A more problematic assault would focus on utilities or satellite and phone systems." CSIS estimates 95 percent of U.S. military communications run through civilian phone networks. An attack on these systems could impede military communications. Cilluffo doesn't believe a cyber-terror incident is imminent, but he doesn't rule it out in the future because members of groups such as Al Qaeda and Hezbollah who have been educated in Western universities are capable of engineering such cyber-attacks. In December, 2001, hackers cracked into a Navy research facility in Washington, D.C. and stole two-thirds of its source code for satellite and missile guidance systems. The Navy claims the source code was an unclassified, older version.

Uncle Sam Wants A Few Good Hackers

It should come as no surprise that Uncle Sam is looking for a few good hackers. That's why Richard Clarke, Bush's former cyber-security czar, addressed thousands attending the 2002 Black Hat Security Briefings in Las Vegas, hosted by Jeff Moss. Clarke pointed a finger of blame at software developers and Internet service providers for the vulnerabilities that plague our nation's networks. Clarke said

> By selling broadband connectivity to home users without making security a priority, telecommunications companies, cable providers, and ISPs have not only opened the nation's homes to attack, but also created a host of computers with fast connections that have hardly any security. There are a lot of people in our country that rely on cyberspace who are not taking responsibility for securing their part of it! The major issue is that companies and organizations who create the hardware, software, and services that make up the Internet, aren't doing enough to secure their products!

In addition to blaming software manufacturers and ISPs for the current rash of security flaws, Clarke singled-out wireless networks as being particularly vulnerable. "Companies throughout the country have networks that are wide open because of wireless LANs! The Department of Defense has already shut down all wireless LANs within the department and in the various military forces."

Figure 8.16 *Uncle Sam wants you! poster*

Clark acknowledged that although few firms admitted it, the Nimda virus in 2001 hit nearly every major financial and banking institution hard, causing nearly $3 billion in damage. The Nimda virus got into computers through vulnerabilities that were known at the time! Nimda didn't spread because the vulnerabilities had not been identified; rather, it spread because patches were not applied. Clarke suggested, "Nimda was so successful not because the system administrators didn't have a chance to apply the patch, but because they wanted to test the patch themselves!" Clarke compared the role of his audience, packed full of security experts, to Winston Churchill and his early warnings of Germany's aerial build-up prior to World War II: "You all have a responsibility to be like Winston Churchill, out there in front of anyone who will listen to say that we are vulnerable. If a cyber war comes, and come it will, we must be like the Royal Air Force and win!"

The IT Pyramid

The third side of the hacker and security pyramid is the IT pyramid. IT (*Information Technology*) is a catchall phrase for any occupation that is remotely computer-related. Hackers who want to compute for a living but who don't have the skills or inclination to go into security are still a hot commodity on the job market. A cursory search on Monster.com reveals a smattering of IT job categories. These are just the tip of the iceberg!

Figure 8.17 *The IT pyramid*

I won't bore you with a laborious description of these positions except to say they have every bit as much impact on your security and privacy as do hackers and security experts. These days you're as likely to be hacked by a company you already know as by some hacker you never heard of!

CHAPTER 9
Media Meltdown

The Politics of Piracy

- ➤ Nobody Owns Cyberspace
- ➤ The Media Meltdown
- ➤ The Media Knot
- ➤ The Z Factor: Warez, Sitez, Crackz, and Piratez
- ➤ Microsoft versus Apple: The Rematch
- ➤ Snitch or Switch
- ➤ Products Too Smart for Their Own Damn Good

From my last book:

> During one frantic week of wheeling and dealing in mid-December 1999, America Online entered into two multimillion dollar pacts—with Circuit City and Wal-Mart—one day after Yahoo! entered into a similar pact with Kmart, and Microsoft invested $200 million in Best Buy. A few months later, AOL announced it was acquiring Time Warner. During the previous year, NBC joined forces with Microsoft, Ted Turner rolled CNN into Time Warner, Michael Eisner bought ABC for Mickey Mouse, and Mel Karmazin sold CBS to Sumner Redstone's Viacom. The only remaining question is who will merge with Barry Diller? These media, Internet, and retail titans all formed alliances for a single reason: Fear!

We now know the outcome of that round of merger-mania and fear. Redstone and Karmazin won't sit in the same room together, AOL Time Warner is $30 billion in debt, Steve Case and Gerald Levin are out of jobs, Michael Eisner is next, and Ted Turner is dumping his AOL stock! In a recent interview, Turner asserted that his personal fortune, once more than $7 billion, has declined 80 percent in value due mainly to the plunge of his AOL Time Warner shares. Turner was the largest single shareholder, with 3.5 percent of all outstanding shares, when AOL began to tank.

The Five-Legged Octopus

Before drawing any hard-and-fast conclusions about the media, it would help to define the media. Prior to convergence and merger-mania, that answer was simple: the traditional media was a five-legged octopus, consisting of

- ➤ Publishing
- ➤ Music
- ➤ Radio
- ➤ Movies
- ➤ Television

The Sixth Leg

The advent of the Internet was akin to the octopus growing a sixth leg! It was a new branch of the old media. From the very beginning, the five legs plotted to control and devour the sixth by merging with it, buying it, and throwing money at it. That's what led to the Internet boom—and bust! Before leaping headlong into new media, it would have been prudent of the old media to ask (and answer) what they were buying into. What was the Internet?

The hallmark of the Internet is convergence. Take the telephone, an ancient technology that predated the media business. The lowly telephone was the technological catalyst that drove the Internet explosion! After all, without modems and landlines, there could be no Internet. The Internet has the power to merge old technologies with new ones by morphing them. For years computers and telephones sat next to each other but had no connection. Overnight, the telephone became the link that connected millions of isolated computers. The nerds emerged from their caves into the light. Suddenly technology was chic!

Nobody Owns Cyberspace

As the Internet kept morphing into different things, it became clear that the sixth leg of the octopus would eventually devour the other five. First came e-commerce, virtual storefronts, and the clicks-and-bricks thing. Next there was MP3, a music-compression algorithm that had the media industry (especially the music business) quaking in its boots. The whiz kids in Silicon Valley chided the old media that they had nothing to fear from new technology—that is, until pirated CD-ROMs of software started popping up on eBay! Everyone eventually figured out that nobody owned cyberspace, but not before the traditional media went broke investing in it!

The Media Meltdown

The Internet is a digital outlet for analog media. The tech sector calls it new media, but that's intentionally vague. So what is the media? It is any technology capable of storing, manipulating, delivering, or displaying information!

The Internet is an outgrowth of the computer, which places the computer at the root of today's media business. What separates the computer from every other machine that preceded it is that it's the only machine ever invented to do nothing. It takes an OS and software for a computer to do something, and today's computers can do virtually anything!

"Computers are now commodities" is a familiar refrain since the tech boom fizzled. Meanwhile, computer peripherals have become the superstars! Attach an ink-jet printer and you have a photo lab, attach a scanner and you have a copier, install a DVD player and you can watch a movie, install a 3D graphics card and you can turn your PC into a gaming machine. Diamonvision billboards, movie theater projection systems, cell phones, PDAs, PVRs, TiVos, iPods, camcorders, cameras, digital cable boxes—computers power the world! Yet the stocks of tech bellwethers such as Intel and Microsoft plunged while the shares of peripheral darlings such as NVIDIA soared. Why? What happened? What really caused the tech bubble to burst? Perhaps this is an oversimplification, but aside from voodoo accounting, shill analysts, crooked CEOs, and cooked books, I believe there are aspects of this story that haven't yet been told.

Broadband: The Internet's Baby

Flash back to the good old days, the Internet boom of the mid-nineties. Based on general consensus, everyone agreed on a simple plan. The content creators (media conglomerates) and content providers (tech titans) would form a partnership to acquire telephone companies, which had been a dead sector for years. The goal was to create an infrastructure to usher in the era of broadband delivery on demand. Thanks to the promise of the "fat pipe" (broadband), you could theoretically come home at four in the morning, turn on the TV, and watch Friends, last night's Yankees game, or Reverend Gene Scott—assuming you'd want to watch anything at four in the morning. Broadband is the Internet's baby! It didn't exist before, and it would never have been invented were it not for the Internet. Broadband was a plot hatched by content providers and content creators—in other words, technology and the media—to control the delivery of digital content.

Napster

Everything was going fine until Napster upset the apple cart! The record labels were already up in arms over MP3, an algorithm that enabled users to compress their audio CD files to a tenth of their original size with no discernable loss in quality.

There were reasonable arguments to be made. MP3 is an archival technology that enables users to back up their music libraries. MP3 would be a boon to the floundering music business because young listeners would be introduced to generations of music that were all but forgotten. Many aging rock stars agreed with this as their record labels rushed to reissue CDs of hits from the sixties and seventies. Queen and Ozzy Osbourne were reborn! The media business remained indifferent to the music industry's objections over MP3 until Napster perked up their ears (a little like the ears on their logo)!

Figure 9.1 *The Napster logo*

Napster was a Perry Mason moment for the media. Silicon Valley was out to screw Hollywood! If technology could enable people to pirate and swap music, the same rules applied to other forms of intellectual property, such as television shows, movies, and books. This was war! The media no longer trusted technology, and the tech companies accused the media of screwing up a business plan that had been years in the works. The marriage was over and the partnership was off!

The Day the Tech Bubble Burst

The NASDAQ peaked at 5048.62 on March 10, 2000 and then tanked. The prevailing wisdom is that a March 20, 2000 research report in *Barron's* magazine predicting a cash crunch triggered the slide. The new economy had to sell its wares to somebody. The old economy was buying, but *Barron's* suggested that the old economy was faltering. The NASDAQ slid more than 200 points that day. The next day, the Fed hiked interest rates for the fifth meeting in a row, and the lockup period for 1999 IPO stock options expired. Suddenly more people were selling tech stocks than buying them!

On April 3, 2000, there was another coup de grace. Microsoft was found guilty of antitrust violations. April 15, 2000—tax day, when profits are traditionally taken and losses are declared—was the straw that broke the camel's back. The NASDAQ closed at 3321 on April 14, 2000. It slid 1727 points from its high of 5048 on March 10, 2000. Thirty-five percent in 34 days!

That's Wall Street's side of the story, and I don't necessarily disagree. But in my humble opinion, the tech bubble actually burst a year earlier on June 1, 1999, the day Shawn Fanning launched Napster! This rudimentary peer-to-peer file-sharing program stopped the media freight train in its tracks. Delivery on demand was suddenly on hold, and broadband, which was almost ready for prime time, now had nothing to deliver. The tech companies and media conglomerates began divesting themselves of phone companies, and the communications sector was the first to tank. The media rallied behind the Recording Industry Association of America (RIAA), which sued Napster for copyright infringement. The RIAA won and put Napster out of business, but a bitter taste has lingered ever since—the media's distrust of technology. The bottom line is that Napster froze progress, and the two biggest casualties were Silicon Valley and Hollywood!

The New-Media Octopus

Which brings us back to the octopus. How many tentacles does the media have today?

> **The Internet**. It took the Internet less than five years to attract a critical mass of 25 percent of U.S. households, compared to seven years for television, eight years for radio, and 28 years for cable. Even as Web surfing has become America's latest passion, eBay is developing a television series.

> **Technology**. This includes computers, software, peripherals, iPods, digital cameras, plasma displays, and high-definition televisions.

> **Communications**. This includes networks, Wi-Fi, cell phones, cable, satellite, DSL, GSP, and OnStar.

> **Video games**. Game publishers generated $9.4 billion in revenues in 2002, compared to $8.3 billion for movie box-office receipts.

> **Advertising**. Five holding companies control 76 percent of the world's advertising market. Online advertising totaled $5.95 billion in 2002. The top 15 Internet ad sellers, such as DoubleClick, account for more than 80 percent of all online ad revenue. Some of Hollywood's hottest directors come straight from Madison Avenue.

> **Publishing**. This includes newspapers, books, magazines, comics, e-books, and sheet music.

> **Music**. This includes records, tapes, CDs, downloads, and audio books.

- ➤ **Radio**. This includes FM, AM, shortwave, CB, Internet, satellite, and cable formats.
- ➤ **Movies**. This includes films, Pay-Per-View, DVD, videotape, and streaming media.
- ➤ **Television**. This includes news, sports, entertainment, Internet, satellite, and cable.

The Media Knot

The old five-legged octopus now has ten legs that are hopelessly intertwined! The media morphed into an unrecognizable knot of commingled partnerships between various sectors that wanted to get in on the Internet boom, broadband, and delivery on demand. It's a little like *The War of the Roses*— bitter divorcees now forced to live under the same roof. Yasser Arafat and Ariel Sharon sharing a beach house in Beirut is the analogy I use to describe the relationship between Silicon Valley and Hollywood.

A groundbreaking and controversial FCC decision in June 2003 relaxed the rules limiting the ownership of TV stations, radio stations, and newspapers by media conglomerates, which bolsters the media knot theory. The FCC proclaimed that decades-old regulations are now obsolete, in part because of the rise of the Internet and other new technologies. FCC Chairman Michael Powell believes that technology offers a wealth of media alternatives that simply were not available a generation ago—the Internet, 802.11 wireless networks, XM and Sirius satellite radio, DIRECTV, hundreds of cable channels, new low-power FM radio, and more magazines and books. "America needs modern rules that take into account the explosion of new media outlets," Powell expounded.

The Z Factor: Warez, Sitez, Crackz, and Piratez

There is one bond that perseveres: piracy is the common enemy of Hollywood and Silicon Valley! Warez (pronounced *wares*, as in software) is a term commonly used to describe illegally distributed software from which copy protection has been removed, if it had any in the first place. In hacker parlance, a "z" is often substituted for an "s." There are warez groups that devote every waking hour to gathering, cracking, and distributing software so others can download it for free. The groups compete to crack the latest software releases first and post them before the competition. Warez can be downloaded on sitez (pronounced *sites*), and they are not restricted to software. There are also warez sitez dedicated to the latest movies, recordings, video games, and porn.

Long before Eminem's second album, *The Eminem Show*, hit the store shelves in 2003, it was the second-most-played CD on computers around the world. That statistic comes courtesy of Gracenote, a company that maintains an online database that identifies a CD by matching the song titles and lengths. Media players such as WinAmp, RealOne, and MusicMatch check this database when a CD is placed in a computer drive so the software can identify the name of the CD and the song titles. This digital Top 40 generally holds few surprises, but when *The Eminem Show* hit Gracenote's chart at number 2 before the CD was even released, it made headlines!

Gracenote CEO David Hyman said, "This is the first time anything unreleased has shown up at number 2." The rapper's label, Vivendi Universal/Interscope, moved the release date up twice to circumvent piracy. The album was already online in MP3 format, but on a busy street corner in New York City the Friday before its long-awaited release, bootleggers were hawking *The Eminem Show* for five dollars a copy on card tables stacked with compact discs.

John Sankus, Jr. is a soft-spoken computer technician who used to work at a Gateway store in suburban Philadelphia. He'll never forget the day in December 2001, when 40 armed Customs agents burst into his workplace and arrested him as a ringleader of DrinkOrDie, a warez group that was a chief target among 100 coordinated raids in the United States and abroad. Sankus is now serving a 46-month stretch in the Allenwood penitentiary on a felony count of conspiracy to commit copyright infringement. Prosecutors accused DrinkOrDie of stealing millions of dollars worth of intellectual property and warned them that the damage is irreversible, despite guilty pleas from Sankus and others, because of the nature of Internet distribution.

Warez groups operate in secrecy, relying on encryption, disguised IP addresses, and invitation-only chat rooms. Their hierarchy is highly structured and broken into two groups. Release groups produce the pirated warez, and courier groups are the worldwide distributors. Government investigators estimate there are roughly 30 major release groups enlisting some 1,500 people around the world. In the DrinkOrDie raids, warrants were served on members in Britain, Australia, Finland, Norway, and Sweden. At least half of DrinkOrDie's members lived outside the United States.

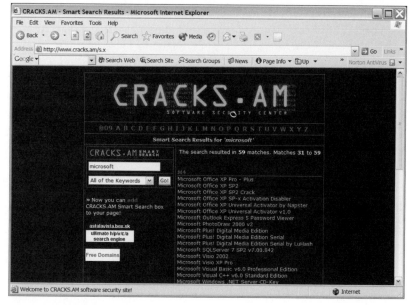

Figure 9.2 *A warez site*

Warez groups specialize in pirating certain types of content. FairLight and Razor1911 are known for pirating video games, FTF and Immortal VCD release Hollywood movies, POPZ focuses on kid's game, and DrinkOrDie was best known for cracking Windows 95 before Microsoft even released it. Warez involves furious competition. Groups race to be the first to release popular movies and titles, but quality is of equal importance. Warez groups often diss each other. Immortal VCD once called a competitor's dupe of *Lilo and Stitch* sub par, describing it as "dark, shaky, and pixilated," and released an improved version of its own.

According to Sankus, DrinkOrDie divided its labor. Suppliers, generally insiders at software companies, provided new versions of software. Crackers, who have the most technically challenging job, strip the program of its copy protection. Testers then make sure the unprotected software works properly. Finally, packers divide the programs into small files and distribute them to release sites. Before moving into a leadership role, Sankus was a tester and a packer for DrinkOrDie.

The Politics of Piracy

The media has proven it will go to any lengths to stem piracy and protect intellectual property, including becoming hackers themselves! In a comical role-reversal with very serious overtones to individual privacy, the entertainment industry is lobbying Congress to consider a proposal that would authorize copyright holders to disable personal computers used for illegal file swapping. A draft bill sponsored by Representatives Howard Berman (CA) and Howard Coble (R-NC) marks the boldest political effort yet by the record labels and movie studios to disrupt peer-to-peer networks. This outrageous measure would permit copyright holders to perform nearly unchecked electronic hacking if they have a reasonable basis to believe that piracy is taking place. Berman and Coble introduced their Orwellian ten-page bill in 2002. Fortunately, it was voted down—unfortunately, nothing can prevent its reintroduction.

At the opposite end of the spectrum, Senator Sam Brownback (R-KS) drafted a bill in 2003 that would scale back the ability of record labels, movie studios, and software companies to use anticopying technology. His bill would regulate DRM (*Digital Rights Management*) systems, grant consumers the right to resell copy-protected products, and require digital media manufacturers to prominently disclose to consumers the presence of anticopying technology in their products. The Brownback bill would require a copyright holder to obtain a judge's approval before receiving the name of an alleged peer-to-peer pirate. That would amend the 1998 Digital Millennium Copyright Act, which enables a copyright holder to force the disclosure of a suspected pirate's identity without a judge's review. The main thrust of Brownback's bill is to slap regulations on digital rights management technology! Brownback said, "My legislation gives the content industry a free hand to create new DRM-enabled business models, but ensures that their success or failure rests in the marketplace, where it belongs—not in Congress!"

Microsoft versus Apple: The Rematch

With so much at stake and no viable solution, it's easy to understand how we got into this mess. The question is how to untangle the media knot. Bill Gates believes that a combination of Palladium and the Windows Media Data Session Toolkit, Microsoft's version of DRM, will win back the hearts and minds of an incredulous Hollywood. But if Microsoft switches sides in the DRM debate, and Palladium is as Machiavellian as its critics claim, will users abandon Windows like rats abandoning a sinking ship? That's the real question!

Figure 9.3 *The iTunes Web site*

Ironically, the first glimmer of hope for consumers since the 1999 Napster fiasco was the launch of Apple's iTunes store in 2003. The revolutionary 99-cents-per-song music download site set the music world, the Internet, and DRM on their collective ear! Leave it to Steve Jobs to get things right. Bill Gates' old nemesis has been on a winning streak. While running Pixar Studios, producer of digital animation classics such as *Toy Story*, Jobs also found time to rescue and reinvent his old alma mater, Apple. First came the transparent iMac, next the revolutionary iPod, then the redesigned LCD iMac, and finally, Jobs' Hollywood coup. The iTunes store single-handedly reopened the floodgates of delivery on demand that had been in a logjam ever since Napster!

Figure 9.4 *The New Media king?* Photo by Moshe Brakha

The iTunes DRM Model

What's so revolutionary about iTunes store?

> ➤ **MPEG-4 AAC**. The AAC (*Advanced Audio Coding*) file format, aka MP4, combines built-in DRM and better audio compression. AAC

audio compression at 96 kbps generally exceeds the quality of MP3 audio compression at 128 kbps according to Dolby Labs, a co-developer of the MP4 standard.

➤ **Copy protection**. Songs sold by the iTunes Music Store cannot be copied onto more than two Macs or shared through a network. The music may be ripped to an unlimited number of CDs, however.

➤ **Royalties**. Artists receive the same royalty per download as they would receive if the same song were sold on a CD.

The runaway success and dramatic popularity of Apple's iTunes Music Store is poised to change everything. In its first month of operation, Apple sold about three million songs at 99 cents each. According to Robin Bloor of Bloor Research,

> The success of iTunes Music Store is even more remarkable if you consider the fact that the service is currently confined to Mac users who make up less than 1 percent of home PC users in the US, and that it does not currently include all music labels. Naturally, Apple is thinking of porting the software to Windows. If you do the math, this could expand the market by a factor of 100, and Apple could be staring a $3 billion a year market in the face. And that's just for the music itself, never mind the iMacs, iPods, and software it could sell!

When rock 'n' roll moved from radio to video, MTV became the hottest force in music. With the iTunes Music Store, Apple may become the next MTV! Thirty days after the launch of the iTunes Music Store, Apple's stock had already risen 25 percent in value. The hackers weren't far behind! Apple's

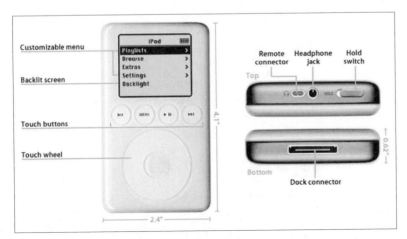

Figure 9.5 *The Apple iPod*

Rendezvous, part of OS X, enables Apple peripherals to share data over a network. Two Mac users with iTunes can share each other's music over a network without actually copying the music files, for example. When one user logs off, the playlist is no longer available to the other. It was only a matter of weeks before hackers tweaked Rendezvous so the software's file-sharing capabilities expanded to the Internet. Although no file copying took place because of the built-in DRM in the AAC file format, thousands of strangers thousands of miles apart could listen to each other's iTunes playlists over the Web. Apple got wind of the hack and released iTunes 4.0.1 within a month. It disabled Rendezvous' capability to share playlists over anything more than a local area network. Apple officially expressed disappointment about how the feature was used, but that's naive. Where there's a will there's a way, and where there's a way there's a hacker. Unfortunately, piracy is here to stay!

Snitch or Switch

Nowadays everyone wants an iPod—even Windows users! It just so happens that Windows users can't download songs from Apple's iTunes Music Store yet. What a coincidence! Windows sites will invariably knock off Apple's DRM model and undercut the price, and iTunes will eventually accommodate Windows users, but that's really beside the point. The point is that DRM has opened a floodgate that could mark an end to the era of Wintel dominance! Microsoft's market share has been slipping due to operating systems such as UNIX, Linux, and Mac OS X, and Intel is losing its foothold because of rival chips from AMD, IBM, and computers such as the iMac!

A few weeks ago I interviewed George Kurtz, the CEO of Foundstone, for this book. Kurtz is familiar with every OS known to man, and when I questioned him about Windows security, George had a startling solution:

Buy a Mac! A veteran Windows user, Kurtz confessed that he recently made the switch to a Mac for personal computing. He finds OS X more elegant than Windows from an aesthetic point of view, and he thinks the UNIX kernel is inherently more stable and secure than Windows NT. George may have a point. All things being equal, OS X historically has required fewer critical updates and security patches than Windows XP has.

George may use a Mac while I use a PC, but over the course of our conversation it became apparent that we use the same keyboard and mouse, Logitech's Cordless Elite Duo MX! I asked George if he was aware that two types of spyware lurk in the software that Logitech installs—Logitech's Desktop Messenger and WildTangent's Game Channel. Unless you opt out,

Figure 9.6 *Logitech Cordless Elite Duo MX*

both programs install by default. George was unfamiliar with them, but he told me he opts out of programs like these automatically because of the likelihood that they contain spyware. So do I, said I! As a general rule, don't install software or drivers unless they're absolutely essential if you're not absolutely certain they aren't spyware.

As an afterthought Kurtz added, "I also run Ad-aware once a week." Ditto, said I! I then described how Ad-aware identified 63 spyware components on

Figure 9.7 *The WildTangent Web site*

my system after I foolishly downloaded and installed WildTangent's 3D visualization for Windows Media Player 9. That's how I became hip to WildTangent. After my conversation with Kurtz, I did more research.

On a WildTangent: Not All Fun and Games

WildTangent is the brainchild of Alex St. John, the superstar who developed DirectX technology at Microsoft. WildTangent began five years ago in Microsoft's Multimedia lab as a Web technology called Chrome. When Microsoft pulled the plug on Chrome, St. John and Jeremy Kenyon, a mathematician and computer systems expert, started working on their own version from scratch.

WildTangent streamlined 3D development, bringing development time down to three or four months for a two- or three-person team, as opposed to two years for 10 people or more. Their Web Driver uses unique compression technology to create virtual bandwidth, speeding up downloads and performance and creating richer multimedia content. It enables quick 3D graphics, sound, and animation in your browser regardless of connection speed, and it actually works! WildTangent has developed some stunning 3D games and screensavers. All you have to do to play is download the Web Driver, a free 860-KB browser plug-in currently available only for Windows.

What's the catch? WildTangent's Web Driver is a sophisticated variation of spyware. Although it isn't technically a Trojan horse, it works and behaves like one. In the background, it harvests information from a computer and transmits the data to WildTangent's Web servers. Web Driver litters Windows Registry with so many entries and your hard drive with so many files and folders that it's a real pain to get rid of them once it is installed. I know from personal experience! WildTangent's Web Driver

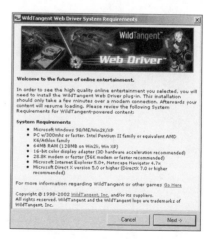

Figure 9.8 *The WildTangent Web Driver system requirements screen*

embedded 63 spyware components on my computer in a single installation, and I had to resort to using System Restore to get rid of it. I document the gruesome details in Chapter 12.

According to WildTangent's own instructions, removal can take anywhere from 10 to more than 30 individual steps, including rebooting your computer and manually deleting files and folders from several locations (including the Windows directory). But if you're like me, you have zero trust in directions supplied by a company that has the gall to purposely install 63 spyware components in a single installation. I just did a search on Google using the phrase "WildTangent spyware" and got 275 hits in 15 seconds! There are horror stories galore from innocent of victims who hosed their computer systems trying to remove WildTangent components. There's even a Web page called "What The Hell Dammit!" (http://empireezine2.tripod.com/computers/whatthe-hell.html) that is devoted to removing WildTangent spyware.

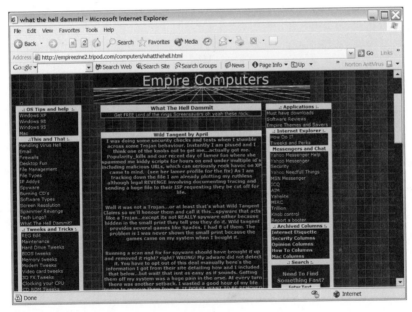

Figure 9.9 *What The Hell Dammit! Web site*

How does WildTangent get away with it? With your permission, and therein lies the rub! In their zeal to download a new screensaver or free game, naïve computer novices click OK and unwittingly fritter away their right to privacy. WildTangent's user agreement reads more like a warning than a EULA.

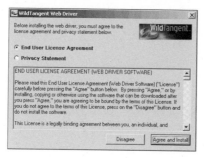

Figure 9.10 *The WildTangent EULA*

WildTangent collects system information through their Web Driver, the software that works with your system configuration to optimize your games based on your particular system. This information is used to upgrade the Web Driver and better optimize Web Driver performance.

The information collected for this purpose includes

➤ CPU speed and type

➤ System memory

➤ Video card configuration

➤ Connection speed

WildTangent also collects game playing information through the Web Driver that is used to determine how users are interacting with the game to determine ways that games may be improved and what features users like and do not like.

The information collected for this purpose includes

➤ Name of the game

➤ Number of game launches

➤ Number of new game starts

➤ Time spent in game

➤ What levels were accessed

➤ Number of purchases versus demo plays

➤ Where the game was downloaded from

WildTangent may share system and game playing information with select third parties on an anonymous basis from time to time.

Who Profits from Selling Your Behind?

WildTangent is in bed with a veritable who's-who of major corporations. This legitimacy combined with the excellence of their technology is what makes WildTangent such a threat!

WildTangent's business partners include

Marketers and advertisers
Anheuser-Busch
BellSouth
Dial
Daimler Chrysler
Gateway
Hyundai
Intel
MCI
Nike
Pepsi
Radio Shack
Sony Electronics
Subaru
Toyota Motor Corporation

TV and film studios
Disney
Fox Sports
FX Networks
Sony Pictures

Digital entertainment
TBS Superstation
The WB
TNT

Portals
AOL Music's WinAmp.com
Flipside Network
GamePro
GameSpy
IGN.com
MP3.com
Shockwave.com
UGO
Uproar
WindowsMedia.com

ISPs
BellSouth
Cablevision
EarthLink
Road Runner
TELUS Mobility
Verizon

OEMs
Compaq
Gateway
Hewlett-Packard
Logitech

Game Publishers
Activision
Electronic Arts
Vivendi Universal

Despite numerous conspiracy theories on the Web claiming that WildTangent is a plot hatched by Microsoft to spy on computer users, and in light of Alex St. John's Microsoft roots, it's notable that Microsoft is absent from WildTangent's partners list. The link to the WildTangent 3D visualization that hosed my PC was on Microsoft's WindowsMedia.com, which is listed as a partner. So is Logitech, maker of the Cordless Elite Duo MX that George Kurtz and I use. After doing further research into WildTangent and Logitech's Desktop Messenger (which is also spyware), I have to conclude George is right. Mac is more secure than Windows! The reason is as obvious as the nose on your face. WildTangent's 3D fun and games and Logitech's Desktop Messenger don't run on a Mac; they run exclusively on Windows!

A Crystal Ball

This just a fantasy, but I can envision the corporate giants in the list of Wild-Tangent's business partners huddled around a crystal ball in a secret room at WildTangent headquarters, watching computer users in their living rooms! And who do you think is right up front? You know who!

The Right Spin on Spyware

I know some of you think I'm being a tad hysterical. That's why I'm going to pass the ball to Steve Gibson when it comes to the subject of spyware. For those of you who don't know, Steve is the founder of Gibson Research and the inventor of SpinRite, the most trusted and widely used disk utility ever written for mass storage data maintenance and recovery. Rated number one since 1988, SpinRite is Gibson's masterpiece, but over the years his name has become synonymous with so much more. Gibson is considered by many to be the first Netizen of the Internet, as well as the conscience of technology. He's the kind of guy who would rather give it away than make you pay. Profits from SpinRite allowed Gibson to develop dozens of free utilities for the masses. There's one more thing you should know: Steve Gibson holds others to his ethical standards!

A few years ago, while assembling a site to help consumers opt out, Gibson encountered something chilling—Web sites that use consumer profiling and tracking technology to invade your privacy! Gibson spoke out (rather publicly, as usual), and because of his standing in the tech community, he rattled a lot of cages. Shortly thereafter, Gibson received the following e-mail from

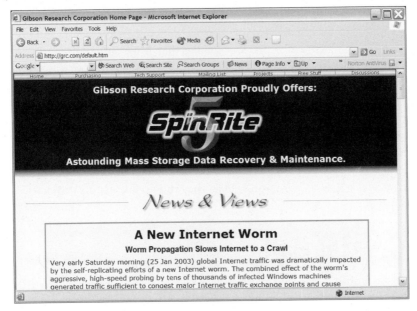

Figure 9.11 *Gibson Research Corporation Web site*

the vice president of marketing for a large streaming-media company that
shall remain nameless.

> Steve,
>
> Would love to chat with you. What is a phone number and a good time
> to chat? We spend a lot of time on the privacy issue and want to be
> sure we understand all concerns. You have very little to fear from
> our technology. While we may be able to suggest you might like
> Miles Davis, we have no idea of any personally identifiable infor-
> mation (e.g. don't know your name, email address, city, state, age,
> gender, etc.).

Several things about this note rubbed Gibson the wrong way. Since his
thoughts had recently been crystallizing about these issues, he took the
opportunity to frame his concerns more coherently.

> Hi [name withheld],
>
> I am somewhat surprised by the depth, strength, and passion of my
> own reactions when I'm told that your company, with which I've
> never had any explicit, deliberate, or overt contact, might be able
> to tell me that the person typing here at this keyboard likes Miles
> Davis. Can't you see that the fact that you don't know my name is

totally irrelevant to the breach of personal privacy you are defending, and from which you are profiting?

Without my knowledge or permission, you quietly monitor and surveil my activities and the choices I make as I move across the Internet. You compile a secret dossier describing my habits, my personal preferences, my search engine queries, my past purchases and spending, and even the contents of many Web forms I have filled out and submitted. Then, having compiled a secret dossier on me--specifically and uniquely me--you deliberately seek to influence me in order to profit from that influence which you now have gained over me.

For the past 25 years I have been an active participant in the creation of the technology we are all using today. I know how it all works, I've had my hands in it, I love it, and I have respect for it.

You don't.

You came along and stole it. You have usurped, raped, and twisted this fundamentally beautiful technology for your own profiteering ends. And in doing so, you have spoiled something wonderful for the rest of us.

I don't want YOU to know ANYTHING about ME, yet you can profile me on a whim, and you see nothing wrong with doing that. Game theorists understand the notion of a zero-sum game: For every winner there's a loser. Physicists understand conservation of macroscopic properties like energy. In both cases they mean that you cannot create something from nothing.

So, if your knowing that I prefer Miles Davis is valuable to you or your clients, from where did that value derive? Value is not created out of thin air. I believe that you have stolen something valuable from me without asking, without my knowledge, and certainly without my permission. You have stolen my unique identity and codified it inside your databases. You have invaded my privacy for your own profit, and what you have taken diminishes me.

...and you want me to say that's okay?

If you are able to "deliver tailored ads to my desktop" for the purpose of increasing the likelihood that I will purchase your client's products instead of someone else's, that's tantamount to seduction through subliminal persuasion. And it is quite properly against the law.

...and you want me to say that's okay?

When I read billboards while driving my car down the freeway, I encounter the same billboards as everyone else. The signage is not "per driver." When I flip through the pages of a magazine, I encounter the same ads as everyone else. The magazine knows nothing about me, and I don't want it to.

When I watch television with my family, I see the same commercials as the rest of my family. But imagine for a moment that your online profiles for my family were able to individually tailor the television commercials we each received, and that everyone had their own televisions in the living room—which we could all see at once. Wouldn't we be curious to see which commercials we each received based upon your Internet profiles of us? Wouldn't some eyebrows be raised in voyeuristic curiosity? And wouldn't that be a fundamental violation of our individual rights to privacy? Yet, isn't this precisely what you're doing and defending, and from which you are profiting?

I believe that what you're doing by "customizing," "targeting," "tailoring," and "identifying" the nameless Internet consumer is fundamentally different from anything that has come before. And I believe that doing this secretly and without my permission is fundamentally wrong, unethical, and evil.

…and I won't say it's okay. I'm going to do everything within my power to explain to consumers exactly what's going on and what's being stolen from us without our knowledge or permission. Then I'm going to create new technology to give them the choice that you have deliberately denied them. I'm going to give them the power to opt out, and to disappear from your radar screens forever.

You wrote, "We spend a lot of time on the privacy issue and want to be sure we understand all concerns." But I don't believe you for a moment. I don't think you have any respect for me or my rights whatsoever. You're profiting from my seduction. How is that good for me?

You wrote, "You have very little to fear from our technology." It is not your technology I fear. I created that technology. It is wonderful and ethically neutral. It is technology in the hands of those who are abusing it that worries me greatly.

Being spied on, being placed under surveillance and tracked around the Internet is not what the technology was designed for. You have taken something wonderful and turned it against us all. That is not okay.

Steve Gibson

Products Too Smart for Their Own Damn Good

Every innovation seems to come with a hidden cost nowadays. Compact discs come with copy protection that prevents them from playing on computers, inkjet cartridges come with chips that prevent them from squirting ink if the cartridge has been refilled, and there are cell phones that won't work if the battery is the wrong brand. I just bought a new G3 cell phone from Sprint, and they have the chutzpah to try to lease polyphonic ring tones to their customers for $1.99 a pop. That's right, lease! After 90 days copy protection kicks in, and the ring tone locks up! Either Sprint thinks its customers are suckers or they're crazy; I don't know which. Polyphonic ring tones are essentially 4-K to 10-K MIDI files that you can download for free all over the Internet. There are millions available; why would I lease *one* ring tone that expires in 90 days for two bucks when I can upload them for free all day long to my Sanyo 8100 phone? Ring-tone kits sell like hotcakes on eBay, and there are Web sites such as http://www.3GUpload.com devoted to uploading cell phone ring tones, games, applications, and animated screensavers. By nickel-and-diming its customers, Sprint is setting itself up to be pirated and hacked!

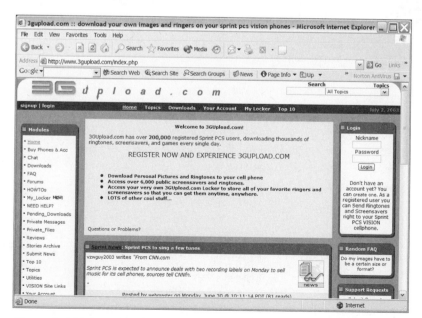

Figure 9.12 *http://www.3GUpload.com*

The Cheap Toothpick Syndrome

Do you remember the story a few chapters back about the restaurant that chintzed on its toothpicks at the expense of its customers? That's the upshot of the media meltdown. Technology, communications, and entertainment that sells the public short and out! The most dangerous variety of the cheap toothpick syndrome is spying on customers and selling their personal information. Unfortunately, this is commonplace. TiVo is typical.

Figure 9.13 *TiVo*

The DVR (*Digital Video Recorder*) is the successor to the VCR. It is essentially a hard drive connected to a TV via the Internet—a stepchild of convergence. DVR makes videotape obsolete by storing 80 hours of recorded programming on an internal hard drive. For a few hundred bucks plus a $12.95 monthly service fee, you can buy a TiVo and never watch another TV commercial again! According to NextResearch, one in five people who own a DVR (such as TiVo or ReplayTV) never watch any commercials. Research also indicates that DVR owners prefer to watch programs recorded on their machine rather than on television itself. Ignoring the networks' painstakingly planned schedules, DVR owners watch programs at their leisure, often oblivious to the channel on which the program originally appeared.

Hollywood and Madison Avenue are in a snit over DVR, as you might imagine. Some even characterize ad skipping as thievery! Jamie C. Kellner, the CEO of Turner Broadcasting, puts it bluntly. "There is no Santa Claus! The free television that we've all enjoyed for so many years is based on watching commercials. If you don't watch commercials, someone is going to have to pay...and it's going to be you!" When prompted, Kellner admitted that, "There's a certain amount of tolerance for going to the bathroom." In 2002, media conglomerates including Viacom, NBC, the Walt Disney Company, AOL Time Warner, and 20th Century Fox slapped SonicBlue, maker of the ReplayTV DVR player, with a federal lawsuit for copyright infringement.

TiVo, SonicBlue's rival, wasn't named in the lawsuit because theoretically, TiVo players can't skip commercials automatically the way ReplayTV players can. In retrospect, there may be another reason why TiVo was excluded from the lawsuit. While everyone was distracted with claims and counterclaims, a light bulb apparently went on in TiVo's head. It was sitting on an untapped gold mine—the viewing habits of its subscribers!

In 2003, TiVo announced it would start selling information about its subscribers' viewing habits to advertisers and broadcasters. The new service will initially provide a quarterly audience-measurement report to track primetime viewing habits, but TiVo eventually plans to use its technology to provide data on consumer patterns for virtually every show and commercial on television.

One way to avoid a lawsuit is join the enemy! This is only hypothetical, but perhaps TiVo wasn't named in the SonicBlue lawsuit because it was playing footsie with the plaintiffs! In my opinion, that's what TiVo has done—misled subscribers, switched sides, and ratted out its customers!

TiVo Privacy Policy: Disclosure of Subscriber Information

3.1 Generally. We disclose aggregated Account Information and aggregated Anonymous Viewing Information and any reports or analyses derived therefrom, to third parties including advertisers, broadcasters, consumer and market research companies and other organizations.

3.6 Factors Beyond Our Control. Your privacy is very important to us. Due to factors beyond our control, however, we cannot fully ensure that your Subscriber Information will not be disclosed to third parties. For example, we may be legally obligated to disclose Subscriber Information to the government or third parties under certain circumstances, or third parties may circumvent our security measures to unlawfully intercept or access your Subscriber Information.

I read the company's privacy policy. Subscribing to TiVo is the equivalent of signing a death warrant on your own privacy. TiVo claims that data is kept in aggregate and doesn't reveal individual information. Where have we heard that before? From every company that's ever been hacked! More to the point, does TiVo have any credibility left after pulling a cheap stunt like spying on subscribers for the almighty buck?

Selling subscription information is TiVo's latest attempt to eke out revenue from a modest subscription base of 703,000 members. TiVo lost $7.9 million in the first quarter of 2003. The company hopes to expand to one million subscribers by 2004. The real question is, will that make a difference? According to Josh Bernoff, principal media analyst for Forrester Research

> TiVo is in a situation where any revenue-generating ideas are important toward the goal of making the company profitable. While the slow economy could make selling research difficult, the authoritative data that TiVo has to offer could pique advertisers' interest. The number of people who want to know the truth about viewing habits and ad skipping is large!

Any way you slice it, TiVo is profiting at the expense of its customers by selling their private information. That is the epitome of the cheap toothpick syndrome!

CHAPTER 10
Badvertising

*How Madison Avenue Killed
Rock 'n' Roll*

I'd like to build the world a home and furnish it with love,

Grow apple trees and honeybees, and snow–white turtle doves.

I'd like to teach the world to sing in perfect harmony,

I'd like to buy the world a Coke and keep it company,

It's is the real thing, Coke is what the world wants today.

—from "I'd Like to Teach the World to Sing" by the New Seekers

On January 18, 1971, Bill Backer, the creative director on the Coca-Cola account for McCann-Erickson, scribbled, "I'd like to buy the world a Coke and keep it company," on the back of a crumpled paper napkin. It was the origin of the most popular television commercial and jingle in advertising history! Backer was flying to London to join two other songwriters, Billy Davis and Roger Cook, to write a Coca-Cola jingle for the singing group the New Seekers. Heavy fog at London's Heathrow Airport forced Backer's plane to land at Shannon Airport in Ireland. After a bumpy flight and lots of circling, the passengers were furious. To add insult to injury, only one hotel was available in Shannon, and the irate travelers were obliged to share rooms with one another. Tempers flared!

The next morning, as the passengers gathered in the airport coffee shop, awaiting flight clearance, Backer noticed that some of the angriest ones were now laughing and sharing stories over bottles of Coke. As Backer recalls in his book, *The Care and Feeding of Ideas* (Times Books, 1993),

> That moment I began to see a bottle of Coca-Cola as more than a drink. I began to see the familiar words, "Let's have a Coke," as a subtle way of saying, "Let's keep each other company for a little while." The basic idea was to see Coke not as it was originally designed—as a liquid refreshment—but as a tiny bit of commonality between all people, a universally liked formula that would help to keep them company for a few minutes.

So Backer turned over a paper napkin and scribbled his now-famous line on the back. Bill Backer was a genius, and in advertising's heyday (the 1970s and 1980s), many a great idea originated on the back of a napkin! On a hillside in Italy in April of 1971, buzzing helicopters filmed 1,200 children wearing the clothes of their various nations, assembled to lip-sync "I'd like to buy the world a Coke" for the rolling cameras. Three months from napkin to jingle to commercial! That's the way advertising was created back then. No committees, no research—only good ideas (and awful ones) that saw the light of day. Believe it or not, "I'd like to buy the world a Coke" was initially a flop! The Coca-Cola bottlers refused to buy airtime for it until Bill Backer prevailed.

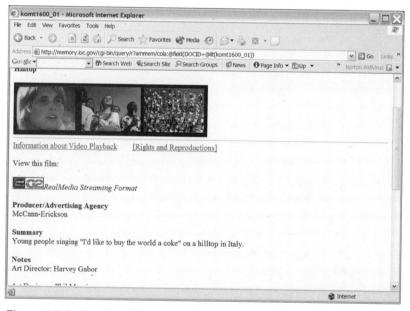

Figure 10.1 *American Memory Coca-Cola advertisement Web site*

I produced television commercials in advertising's heyday. My first job was at Jerry Ansel Studios, a carriage house on East 38th Street that was converted into a film studio. Jerry was a one-man band—producer, director, cameraman, and editor. All of the equipment necessary to shoot commercials was under that roof. Fueled by piping-hot pots of Melita espresso, Jerry hardly ever slept. He literally shot commercials around the clock. Jerry was so accustomed to gazing through the viewfinder of his Arriflex camera that his right eye was fixed in a permanent squint!

I remember Hill, Holliday, Connors, and Cosmopulos—not agency personnel, but the actual guys after whom the agency was named—flying down

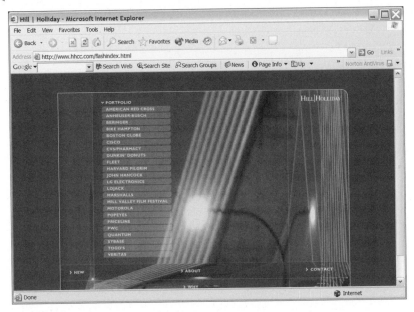

Figure 10.2 *The Hill | Holliday Web site*

from Boston on the 6 a.m. Eastern shuttle. Jerry and I would pick them up at LaGuardia airport, and by the time we hit the Holland Tunnel, Jerry and the boys would have whipped up a new spot or ad campaign. And we'd stay there and shoot it until it was done—for days if necessary!

Animatics

Research slowly changed all that. A few years later, in addition to giving production companies a storyboard to bid on, ad agencies began to produce crude animations of the proposed commercial, called *animatics*. If you were an art director, copywriter, creative director, producer, or director, you hated animatics. Their only purpose was to second-guess your creativity!

Advertising agencies are split into two units that often conflict—the creative department and account management. Account executives are generally MBAs who have known the clients since college. Their job is to do market research, crunch numbers, and hold the clients' hands. The account executives used to use animatics, which they showed to focus groups, as a way of reigning in the crazies in the creative department. That's why we hated animatics!

The Day Elvis Died

I was working on Madison Avenue at D'Arcy, McManus, & Masius the day Elvis died. I stepped off the elevator at 285 Madison and saw the startling headline, "The King Is Dead!" on the cover of *The Daily News*. It didn't occur to me then, but Elvis' death and animatics are inexorably linked. Research killed creativity, and Madison Avenue killed rock 'n' roll!

Mnemonics

Nobody appreciates the importance of memories more than Madison Avenue. The job of advertising is to create Kodak moments to evoke memories of a particular product. However, messing with people's memories by associating rock classics with products is not only a cultural offense, it's an indication of how far creativity has sunk in the ad biz since Bill Backer's era. By sucking the blood out of old rock hits instead of composing original classics like "It's The Real Thing," the true nature of the beast has been revealed. Creatively bankrupt, Madison Avenue has become a cultural vampire!

I knew the Little Rascals personally! I don't want to think of Vioxx when I hear *It's a Beautiful Morning*. And when Vertical Horizon sings *The Best I Ever Had*, I don't want to think of a damn Nissan pickup truck! I think Madison Avenue is playing mind games, and I consider it an invasion of my privacy! The list of rock stars who have sold their souls goes on and on.

➤ Bob Seger, *Like a Rock*, Chevy Trucks

➤ Led Zeppelin, *Rock and Roll*, Cadillac CTS

➤ REO Speedwagon, *Roll with the Changes*, General Motors

➤ Jethro Tull, *Thick as a Brick*, Hyundai

➤ Sting, *Desert Rose*, Jaguar

➤ Meatloaf, *Paradise by the Dashboard Light*, General Motors

➤ Celine Dion, *I Drove All Night* (Roy Orbison cover), Chrysler

I just deleted all of my Sting MP3s! Seriously, I don't want to hear another song from these artists ever again. Dolling up commercials with rock classics began with Microsoft, oddly enough, when they used the Rolling Stones'

Start Me Up as the signature soundtrack for their Windows 95 launch. Microsoft's bold (and expensive) foray into rock 'n roll was reported as hard news at the time. Then, in 1997, Wieden and Kennedy used the Beatles' *Revolution 1* in a Nike commercial. I didn't object to either of those spots because they were musical breakthroughs. I also enjoyed the original Bob Seger *Like a Rock* Chevy truck campaign.

Napster Nips Madison Avenue

Instead of quitting while they were ahead with a handful of classic commercials, Madison Avenue cannibalized the formula ad nauseum. Now every hemorrhoid treatment has its own rock 'n' roll track! The economic rationale for this actually can be traced back to Napster. In the past couple of years, CD sales plummeted by more than 100 million units. 785 million CDs were sold in 2000, compared to just 681 million last year. Because more people are downloading and sharing music online, desperate pop stars and music labels are licensing their hits to Madison Avenue to offset losses from piracy!

Since advertising has become yet another tentacle of the media, this should come as no surprise: five holding companies control 76 percent of the world advertising market. Is it a coincidence that five media conglomerates control 80 percent of the world's entertainment, and five tech companies control 85 percent of world's technology? Or is some kind of pattern emerging here? I'll leave the conspiracy theories to others.

The Silver Lining

Nothing is less creative than being derivative! But while Madison Avenue was killing rock 'n' roll, a handful of agencies bucked the trend by using the same formula to break new ground in the Bill Backer tradition. Vinny Picardi of Deutsch LA reversed the formula, for example. His Mitsubishi campaign turned unknown songs into hits! Dirty Vegas' *Days Go By* might have slipped through the cracks had it not been featured in a Mitsubishi Eclipse commercial. That spot boosted the obscure song onto the music charts and helped it nab a Grammy nomination for Best Dance Recording. Scott Shannon, the morning DJ and program director for New York's WPLJ, heard it on TV and said, "Hey, what's that?"

Volkswagen caught the bug too, putting an unheard-of musician named Ben Neill in its commercials. Neill calls it, "A real convergence between a brand, ad agency, and record company." Neill has made music industry history by becoming the first person to put out an original collection of ten songs written for commercials, aptly titled *Automotive*. His producers at Six Degree Records claim the VW spots are pushing CD sales, and Volkswagen is considering selling the CD at its dealerships.

Advertising's Second Heyday

The Internet boom marked advertising's second heyday! I haven't witnessed as many innovative spots since the golden age of Alka Seltzer's "Some spicy meatball," Volkswagen's "Think small," and Coke's "It's the real thing." For the first time in decades market research took a back seat to creativity once again! My friends in the business tell me it was reminiscent of the good old days, only this time the client wasn't some stodgy frat boy from the Midwest. He or she was a twenty-something multimillionaire from Silicon Valley who had no qualms about pushing the envelope. That was the mandate for ad agencies during the Internet boom. So many IPOs vied for airtime that advertising's primary mission was to cut through the clutter!

The Stuart Principle

To me, the most compelling character on television in the late 1990s wasn't a cast member from *Friends* or *Sex and the City*, or even Tony Soprano! It was Stuart, the punk office boy who tried so desperately to fit into straight society in the hilarious Ameritrade commercials. His clueless boss, Mr. P, needed Stuart to show him the ropes. Stuart represented every geek in Silicon Valley who made good! The ad's subliminal message was, "Technology makes everything easier, but you old fogies have to trust us to benefit from it!"

Figure 10.3 *Stuart from the Ameritrade commercial*

Stuart was the brainchild of Ogilvy & Mather New York. According to Ameritrade's vice president of marketing, Peter Horst,

> Rather than tightly scripted marketing messages, these ads were largely improvised. There was no storyboard, no script; we just hired some actors, told them some points we wanted them to

hit—eight bucks a trade, free research, demonstrate that it's quick and easy—and it was all improv from there. I've done millions of ads and this was most unusual. From a client's perspective, it was a little nerve-racking!

The result, directed by Dewey Hicks, was a spontaneous spot with tongue planted firmly in cheek. Mr. P asks office-worker Stuart, caught in the act of photocopying his face for a party invitation, for some help setting up his online Ameritrade account. As Mr. P gingerly pecks away at his Web browser, Stuart eggs him on with a little chicken dance and utters the unforgettable phrase, "Catch the wave of the future, my man. Let's light this candle!" I think Hollywood really missed the mark by not making a buddy flick featuring Stuart and Mr. P. I can envision it now: Stuart and Mr. P are at a rave, Mr. P flips out on Ecstasy, and Stuart calmly talks him down.

The Day of Reckoning

Stuart was indicative of a trend. Madison Avenue flexed creative muscles it hadn't used in 20 years during the Internet boom! Who can forget the Jujube commercial created for E*Trade by Goodby, Silverstein & Partners? A junior exec sits across from his boss, enumerating the reasons why he should get a raise. The boss is fixated on his bowl of Jujubes. The old man thinks to himself, "The blues and the reds are the kings and queens of Jujubes. The greens and the yellows are like peasants. Will there be a revolution one day?" He looks up and notices the young man waiting for an answer, so he picks up his bowl and offers, "Jujube?"

Captain Kirk slammed poetry for Priceline.com, Outpost.com shot gerbils through cannons, and Yahoo!, one of the few companies to survive the bursting bubble, still airs brilliant commercials today. But the Internet bubble did burst, and there came a day of reckoning—the 2001 Super Bowl. Forty percent of the commercials aired during the 2000 Super Bowl were for emerging dot-coms that had gone belly-up! E*Trade marked the historic occasion with its classic Sergio Leone-esque "Invest Wisely" commercial. A monkey riding a donkey ambled down the center of an abandoned Western ghost town full of boarded-up storefronts of shuttered dot-coms. The monkey peered down, and what did he spot? The remains of the tattered, discarded Sock Puppet! A simple two-word voiceover resonated with the truth, "Invest wisely."

Testing

"Invest Wisely" not only commemorated the end of the Internet boom, it also marked the end of a creative boom on Madison Avenue! The pendulum in the battle over creativity versus research swung once again, but this time there was a new ingredient—technology!

Madison Avenue has been doing market research since time immemorial. By the time animatics rolled around when I was producing commercials, research was a burgeoning industry. But there were still ways to get around research creatively. The trick was to produce a down-and-dirty spot for the approximate cost of producing an animatic and conducting the focus groups. When I worked in ad agencies, the copywriters, art directors, and creative directors constantly badgered me to devise ways to beat the account executives to the punch! That generally entailed convincing a rising director or photographer to do a test spot for cost, with the promise of landing the full-blown job if the concept tested well. Half the time, test spots obviated the need for research because the powers that be (clients and agency heads) knew viscerally whether or not a concept worked.

Suppose the bubble never burst. Suppose delivery on demand arrived on schedule and the Internet sector thrived. I believe research would have still overshadowed creativity in advertising today because technology and information are such a combustible combination! Technology transformed information into a commodity worth big bucks. The same companies that gave us those great commercials in the late 1990s—tech companies and ad agencies—were developing technology that spies on us now! Banks and credit card companies are repositories of financial information, insurance companies are repositories of medical information, and Madison Avenue is a repository of our consumer information.

Laws provide a modicum of privacy when it comes to medical and financial records and our terrorist quotient as assigned by the Department of Homeland Security. But no such law prevents the sale of personal data collected by Madison Avenue. Clients are clamoring to buy consumer information harvested by technology and filtered through Madison Avenue. That's what market research has become—the buying, selling, and trading of personal information unwittingly provided by us!

How Advertising Became Badvertising

Technology and Madison Avenue are a lethal mix to privacy! Coupons and sweepstakes that are pretenses to profile and target us, junk faxes, junk mail, spam, telemarketing calls, adware, cookies, Web bugs, pop-ups—they're all byproducts of advertising. That's why I call it *badvertising*. Madison Avenue has become one big database, and presence awareness technology is waiting in the wings. The marketers and information brokers already know where we live, what we like, and who we are. It's only a matter of time before they know our comings and goings too! Computer chips have become so miniscule and cheap that they're weaving them into fabrics. One day in the not-too-distant future, billboards will suddenly start talking to you when you walk down the street! Just like they pitched Tom Cruise in *Minority Report*, remember? That's what Madison Avenue is cooking up!

Digital Marketing

Madison Avenue and the Web have a symbiotic relationship. The Internet was financed by advertising! Without it, the free Internet couldn't exist. Online advertising totaled $5.95 billion in 2002. Although it was down 14 percent from the previous year, Madison Avenue depends on that revenue stream. Fifteen digital marketing companies with serious-sounding names, such as DoubleClick, Mediaplex, CoreMetrix, and aQuantive (formerly Avenue A), control and generate 80 percent of all online ad sales and revenues.

DoubleClick, the Internet advertising giant, recently sold its North American media sales division to L90, a former competitor, for $9.4 million plus incentives. L90 immediately changed its name to MaxWorldwide. (I guess L90 didn't sound serious enough.) Both companies sold online ad-delivery and tracking technology to advertisers, while selling an advertising inventory on behalf of a network of Internet publishers.

The deal solidified an emerging strategy for both companies. It enabled DoubleClick to concentrate on its advertising technology and data-analysis tools and move out of ad sales, while L90's network expanded to more than 1,000 sites, including the 850 it acquired from DoubleClick. Perhaps this corporate shell game provides plausible deniability, but in my opinion it's a smokescreen. DoubleClick is in the business of harvesting personal informa-

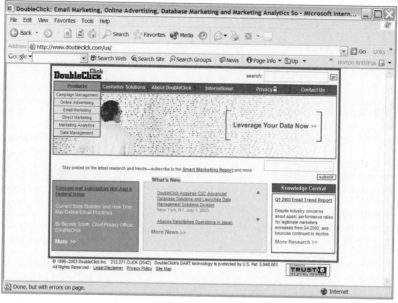

Figure 10.4 *The DoubleClick Web site*

tion and profiling and targeting consumers. Which company sells the banner ads and which develops the technology is really irrelevant!

Ad servers place cookies on computers that track your Web-surfing habits. These companies claim the function of their cookies is to regulate the type and amount of advertising we receive. Baloney! Because of the huge networks these advertisers serve, their cookies have the capacity to identify and shadow us!

Following is an excerpt from DoubleClick's Database Marketing Statement:

> With more than 3.5 billion transactions from more than 90 million U.S. households, DoubleClick's Abacus Alliance Database is the largest proprietary database of consumer transactions used for target marketing purposes. By combining transactional data with advanced statistical modeling, database marketing can help marketers target the potential consumers that are most likely to buy their products or services.

> For consumer-focused marketers who are looking for sophisticated modeling techniques and a large universe of quality names to increase their revenue, Abacus Catalog Alliance is a blind alliance of 1,800 merchants offering shared data representing over 90 million households.

DoubleClick sells names, addresses, e-mail addresses, phone numbers, brand preferences, buying patterns, and other personal information. You just heard it from the horse's mouth!

The Mousetrap

Twenty-five to 30 billion ads bombard weary Web surfers each week, and the future looks grim. Research firm GartnerG2 projects that online advertising will more than double by 2005. It isn't a black-and-white issue, either. Even those who detest pop-up banners concede that Web advertising helps finance the Internet. But with each new generation of technology, online ads grow more intrusive and deceptive. Today's ads either pose as something they're not, contain noncommercial content, or bombard us with pyrotechnic excess. Here's what Web surfers face:

> ➤ Standard banner ads stay inside the primary browser window.
> ➤ Pop-up and pop-under ads appear in new browser windows that are stripped of toolbars and menus.
> ➤ Interstitial ads appear after you click a link but before you see the next page.
> ➤ Transitional ads pop up in a separate window between two pages.
> ➤ Superstitial ads move across a Web page like a projected animation.

A new variety of pop-up ads mimic a dialog box. Web surfers are tricked into clicking the OK button to dismiss a system message, only to be drawn into an abyss of new pop-up ads. Most invasive of all is the so-called *mousetrap*. It breaks your browser's Back button, disables the Close box, and replicates new windows faster than you can close them! The sleazy underbelly of the Internet is rife with spawning technology. You can encounter it anywhere, but avoiding porn sites, gambling sites, warez sites, and spam links will limit your exposure.

Why do advertisers employ invasive technology? Because it works! Unfortunately, the most intrusive ads grab the customers' attention (just like in conventional advertising). In reality, the Web sites and advertisers that employ invasive technology are rewarded for using these techniques. You can block most ads by disabling graphics, Java, JavaScript, and Flash in your Web browser, but that's like throwing the baby out with the bath water! In the process, your whole interactive Web experience would go down the drain. That's why ad-blocking programs such as AdSubtract, AdBlocker, and Web-Washer have become so pop-up-ular (pardon the pun) of late. As recently as

2001, analysts found that three-quarters of the Web surfers surveyed didn't even know what ad-blocking software was.

Ad Blocking

Ad-blocking programs function as proxy servers and run in the background on a PC. The software examines the URL that a Web browser requests, checks it against entries in a frequently updated database of ad servers, and drops the request for ad content if it finds a match. Some programs also use pattern-matching algorithms that can identify windows and images of known ad shapes and sizes. In most cases Web pages load 25 to 50 percent faster without ads. Ads litter your hard drive with temporary files and tracking cookies, hog resources, and consume bandwidth. A good ad-blocking program will not only free up bandwidth and disk space, it will help protect your privacy!

The phrase "ad blocker" returned 93,600 hits on Google in less than a second. Several fine ad-blocking programs are available. WebWasher and Pop-Up Stopper are well rated, and both are free. Be aware of spyware that masquerades as ad-blocking software, however. The Alexa Toolbar (now owned by Amazon) has a notorious reputation as spyware, for example.

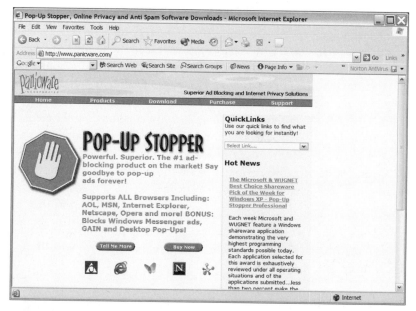

Figure 10.5 *Pop-Up Stopper Web site*

Before installing any program, especially freeware or shareware, always check http://www.spywareinfo.com or http://www.spychecker.com first to see whether the program is listed in their spyware databases.

And remember: you'll find links to Spy Checker, numerous references in this book, and utilities like anti-spy tools and personal firewalls on the *Invasion of Privacy* homepage at http://www.mjweber.com/iop/privacy.htm

The Advertising Police

Greg Stuart, the head of the Interactive Advertising Bureau, an online advertising trade association, insists, "Users must accept the quid pro quo of advertising. They're getting something for free or at a reduced cost. Blocking ads violates that implied contract!" He must be talking to Jamie Kellner, the CEO of Turner Broadcasting, who used the same lame rationale about ad skipping and TiVo. Baloney!

Are you obligated to read every single ad in a magazine or newspaper or watch every commercial on television? Of course not! And Internet ads are more intrusive and offensive than advertising in any other media. Suppose you were reading your favorite magazine and when you turned the page, one of those perfumed inserts popped up and squirted you in the eye. That's what some Internet advertising reminds me of!

For every technology, there's a counter-technology. Some sites aggressively block ad blockers! In 2001, a German company called mediaBEAM developed AdKEY, software that knows if a browser has loaded ad graphics. If AdKEY determines a visitor is using ad-blocking software, it prevents them from entering the site. Shortly thereafter, a German hacking group called the Anti-AdKEY Initiative released details on how users could counter mediaBEAM's technology. The hackers, who mocked the system as "amateurish," said they were able to compromise AdKEY with only a few hours of experimentation and posted their workaround across the Internet. Some things will never change. That's what I love about hackers!

I personally don't block most ads. I allow banners ads, skyscrapers, and animations. I use ZoneAlarm Pro, which has a powerful array of privacy features, so I could block them if I chose. I don't because I love advertising. What I truly detest is badvertising!

CHAPTER 11

Practical and Tactical Digital Defense (Part 2)

An eBay Version of Rocky

> Don't Get Mad. Get Even!

In ancient Rome, Caligula rigged auctions by employing shills to drive up his bid prices. Two millennia later, a flim-flam man pulled the same trick on eBay. His shills drove the bid price of an abstract painting by the artist Diebenkorn, which later turned out to be a forgery, to a mind-boggling $135,805. Fortunately, eBay got wind of the scam and pulled the plug on the auction before any bidders got burned. In 2002, Jason Eric Smith also got swindled on eBay. But unfortunately for Jason, this time eBay couldn't do diddly-squat.

Smith was a 21-year-old college student at the University of New Orleans studying to be a teacher. Making ends meet can sometimes be a struggle, which is how Jason stumbled upon eBay. He's had a lifelong passion for all things (Apple) Macintosh, and he discovered he could augment his income by buying and auctioning Mac computers and peripherals.

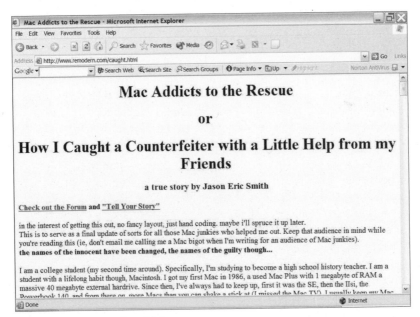

Figure 11.1 *Remodern BBS*

Some names have been changed to protect the innocent and those not yet proven guilty.

The word "con" derives from the word "confidence." Smith had a good thing going on eBay until a con man tricked Jason into trusting him. What happened to Jason could have happened to anyone; it's what he did about it that sets him apart! Here's Smith's story in his own words, as they appear on http://www.remodern.com/caught.html.

Mac Addicts to the Rescue, or How I Caught a Counterfeiter with a Little Help from My Friends
by Jason Eric Smith

I am a college student (my second time around). Specifically, I'm studying to become a high school history teacher. I am a student with a lifelong habit, though—Macintosh. I got my first Mac in 1986, a used Mac Plus with 1 megabyte of RAM and a massive 40-megabyte external hard drive. Since then, I've always had to keep up—first it was the SE, then the IIsi, the PowerBook 140, and from then on, more Macs than you can shake a stick at. (I missed the Mac TV.) I usually keep my Mac for about six months, and then resell it and move up. I almost always buy used, so don't get any ideas about me being rich.

Since I went back to being a student again, I've been selling Macs more regularly, picking up good deals on used Macs locally and then reselling on eBay. I've been doing this for about two years now. It's relatively easy, taking about an hour each day, and it usually pays the rent. In November, when the new PowerBooks came out, I decided I was going to buy one for myself as an early Christmas present. It would come in handy for taking notes in class and finishing up a presentation I needed to do on the New Orleans school system. The day they were announced I ordered a nice new PowerBook G4 867 and found it on my doorstep only a few days later.

It was a beautiful machine! If you've never played with one in person, you won't believe it. I played with it for a couple of days, and took it to school to take notes and do research on. The more I used it, the more I loved it. But it was just too much to be carrying around. $2300 in my backpack had a tendency to make me a little nervous. I decided maybe I should turn it around and pick up an iBook. My girlfriend and I decided we would use the extra money to donate to some charities for Christmas. So on November 19th, up on eBay it went, along with an Airport Base Station and a bunch of other knickknacks. I set a buy-it-now price on a whim for $2950. The next morning I checked my auction, and a couple of bids had been placed, so the buy-it-now option was gone. Checking my e-mail, I got a couple of questions about the computer and, much to my surprise, an offer to buy it for $2900 from Steve M., a dad with a lucky son in college who was going to be getting a PowerBook for his birthday. Steve wanted to pay for it COD, which was no problem. It's actually how I usually sell things.

I called him on the phone number he gave to ask a couple of questions and make sure everything was on the up and up. He reiterated that he was buying it as a last-minute present for his son and, since it was already set up as a package, he thought it was a good deal. Not to mention the Chicago Apple stores were still out of stock. I got home from school, packed up my PowerBook and accessories, and off they went FedEx overnight to Chicago, never to be seen again.

At 10:21 a.m. on November 21st, a man going by the name of Paul S. signed for my two packages and gave the driver an official cashier's check from LaSalle Bank for $3052.78. The check made it back to my doorstep the next morning. I went to the bank, deposited the check and withdrew enough to go ahead and pay my rent and pick up a couple of household items. I sent an e-mail to Steve to make sure he got everything and to check that nothing had been damaged in shipping. No reply. As the old saying goes, no news is good news, right?

My girlfriend and I went away for Thanksgiving, and when we got back on Friday, I had a message from my bank. The branch manager called to let me know she had a returned item for $3052.78 and that my account was now in the negative. Seriously in the negative! No problem, I thought, I'll just call Steve and see what's up. So I dialed his number. In the back of my mind I expected a "this number has been disconnected" message. Instead I got an answer; the voice sounded identical to Steve, so I asked if Steve was there.

"Oh, Steve, yeah, that's my cousin. He's out of town for Thanksgiving, you know. He'll be back Tuesday."

"Can I leave a message for him?"

I left my information and asked that he return my call. That little voice in the back of my mind let out a sigh and an "uh-oh." The voices were the same, right? Was I being scammed? Well, if I was, I certainly wasn't going to let the weekend go by without doing a little investigating.

I started off with the information I had. His AOL e-mail address, his phone number, and the address I shipped the computer to. The AOL address didn't yield anything. Doing a reverse lookup on the address (thanks to whitepages.com), I got three names and phone numbers, none of which matched anything I had. The phone number didn't give me anything. I finally found a way to look up the exchange on the number to see if it was a cell phone or a landline (by using FoneFinder).

It came back as Nextel, and I wanted to scream. There really isn't anything you can do with a cell phone number. There are no directory services; the cell phone companies won't give out any information; and that's that. I called Nextel and pleaded with them. The customer service rep I spoke with seemed more confused than anything. He kept asking me what my Nextel phone number was and why I suspected someone was fraudulently billing to my account. I calmly explained at least three times that I was not a Nextel customer, that I was just trying to get an address for another customer I suspected has defrauded me, etc. I finally gave up on Chris from Nextel.

I was at a dead end! I'd just sent my $2300 laptop, my Airport Base Station, and a load of stuff to somebody I didn't know, and all I had to show for it was a bill from FedEx for overnight shipping and a returned cashier's check. It's hard to sleep comfortably knowing some asshole has your Mac and is doing God knows what with it.

Sunday the first of December, I sprang into action full force. I called for help! I knew I wasn't going to get anywhere with this on my own, so I figured I might be able to get some help from some bulletin boards. I posted my tale of woe and call for assistance on every Mac bulletin board I could think of. I hoped that somebody who worked for Nextel or some fellow Mac addict like myself might be willing to bend the rules a little. I wanted this guy's address, and I wanted it bad. I was already pricing flights to Chicago and putting my professors on notice that I might have to miss a little class. I may have made an error in trusting this person, but I'm not someone you want to have that happen to. I will get you. I will hunt you down, and I will bring a baseball bat with me!

Figure 11.2 *Photo of baseball bat*

I got more replies than I could keep up with. Everyone wanted to know what they could do to help, or at least offer support. Well, everyone except one guy who just wanted to let me know how incredibly stupid he thought I was. He said he'd never have accepted a counterfeit anything. But I think a 102:1 great-person-to-jerk ratio is pretty good. Several people living in Chicago offered their assistance, be it in gathering information or even forming a tough guy squad if necessary!

The most important reply I got was a pointer to an online PI service that does reverse lookups on cell phones (Cell Phone Magic). I was already beyond broke, but I figured $85 more wouldn't kill me. Twelve hours and

$85 later, I had a name, an address, and a landline phone number for this guy. The name and his AOL e-mail were eerily close; actually, with a last name like his, it would be pretty weird if it didn't match up. I couldn't believe it. A Chicago resident named Christmas had just ruined my Christmas! I expected William Faulkner to come popping out of the pantry at any moment and laugh at me.

I was now ready to call the police. I called the Chicago police department and filed a report. I gave the operator all of my information, including Mr. Christmas' real name and address. "A detective will contact you within one to two weeks. Thank you." One to two weeks?!? I found this guy. I'd done all the work already! All they had to do was go pick him up. I'd even gone ahead and called FedEx and spoken to the Chicago station manager, and was assured that the driver would cooperate in identifying this guy if necessary. All they had to do was pick him up. In one to two weeks he could be gone. And all the while my precious PowerBook was being used by somebody completely undeserving of a Mac! I know in my heart that Christmas is really a PC guy.

I was furious that the Chicago PD wasn't going to do anything about this. If they were anything like the New Orleans PD, one to two weeks was likely to turn into never! I figured I'd call Mr. Christmas myself. Let him know I was going to give him a chance to fix this and, I thought, maybe at least scare him. Let him know he was dealing with someone who would track him down no matter what, even if I had to make a deal with the Prince of Darkness to do it. Mr. Christmas said he didn't even know what e-mail was. Obviously a PC user!

I kept checking the message boards. Maybe someone would have a better idea. I called the local FBI field office. Agent Jones was very understanding, but let me know that even though this crossed state lines, the field office didn't take anything involving less than $5000. "Try the Chicago PD."

I kept everyone on the Mac boards updated as best I could. On Tuesday I got a useful reply: "Try the Secret Service; counterfeiting is their jurisdiction." I made my way to the under-renovation Federal Building here in New Orleans. After walking down several dark, scary hallways I found myself at the door of Agent Keith L. Keith came out and heard my case. I had brought copies of all the e-mails between myself and Steve M./Paul S./Mr. Christmas, a copy of the check, and the call journal I had started keeping. Agent L. told me the same thing the FBI did. "It falls under our jurisdiction, but we can't take the case." He wanted to let me know that he really felt for me. Thanks! I left the office determined to call and bother him and the Chicago PD every day for the rest of my life, or at least until Christmas was behind bars.

Finals were fast approaching. It's not very easy to concentrate on school when all you can think is that all of your student loans for the next semester are going to cover this counterfeit check. That, and the fact that some grubby criminal has your PowerBook. Tuesday night I got an e-mail from someone who had seen my story posted on O'Grady's PowerPage, a PowerBook enthusiasts' site. George D. had seen the story and thought it sounded eerily similar to his. I called him, we compared notes, and turns out it was the same guy! George forwarded me all of his e-mails. Everything was the same, word for word. It was like Mr. Christmas just copied and pasted and magically made money. George was in it worse than I was, though, and he had completely given up. He was out $6000 and two computers. He also let me know that there were more victims. He'd talked to at least three other people who had been taken by the same guy, all of whom had just given up. I was not going to give up! That night I dreamed of Mr. Christmas and a baseball bat, some duct tape, and roofing nails.

Wednesday morning I decided I was going to Chicago. I set up another eBay auction under my girlfriend's account, this time for the same computer but from a different city. Three hours later, lo and behold, I received an e-mail from eBay user xxxxxx55 (the same one) asking me if I'd like to sell the computer right now for $2500. Oh yes, I'd love to sell the computer; I'll even be there when it gets delivered to make sure it gets "set up properly."

He e-mailed me a new address and phone number, and the phone number again traced back to the same address for Mr. Christmas. I called the Secret Service and the Chicago PD, pleading; all they had to do was be there when FedEx dropped off the package. It was a guaranteed hit. He'd have another counterfeit cashier's check; all they'd have to do was arrest him! "Sorry, Detective McDonaugh will be out until next Wednesday. Can I take a message?" Fine, if the cops won't do it, I decided I'd just Priceline a ticket and be waiting next door when it got dropped off. So I'd know what kind of neighborhood I was looking at, I asked for help again in the Mac boards. Two Chicago residents replied, and the next morning, courtesy of Tim, I had 23 pictures of the house, the cars in the driveway (with license plate numbers) and the neighborhood. I started planning my trip. I decided I'd leave on Saturday, have the package delivered on Monday, and make it back just in time to screw up on all my finals!

On Friday, in preparation for my trip to Chicago, I mapped the address for Mr. Christmas to see how close it was. As I looked at the map, it hit me. The address wasn't in Chicago. It was in a suburb, Markham. I Googled for the Markham police, and 5 minutes later was talking to a very enthusiastic Sergeant K. I had hit the jackpot! The drop was outside of Chicago jurisdiction and therefore outside of their inattentiveness as well. Sergeant K. informed me he loved this kind of thing and even had a UPS and FedEx uniform ready. He'd call FedEx and they would set it up for Tuesday. I was certain I was dreaming. After talking to two detectives in Chicago, an FBI field agent, an agent in the New Orleans field office of the Secret Service, an agent with the L.A. Secret Service and having a conference call with a large group of agents from the Chicago Secret Service, I finally was getting somewhere! And I didn't even have to stand on someone's doorstep with a baseball bat to do it.

I spent the entire weekend on pins and needles. What if Mr. Christmas figured something out between now and Tuesday? All would be lost. I wouldn't even get the chance to confront him on my own. On Monday I spoke with Sergeant K. to make sure everything was ready to go. I had sent him a package with all of my documentation (he didn't have e-mail), and I tried to explain what all the e-mail meant as best I could. He had worked everything out with FedEx, and they were set for the delivery on Tuesday.

I called my brother in Nashville and had him send the package. I set everything up to come from there so Mr. Christmas wouldn't get suspicious. I could barely sleep Monday night. All I could think about was something going wrong and my only chance at getting this guy being missed. I wanted to update everyone on the Mac boards, but I had to keep it quiet until I knew something was going to happen.

Tuesday afternoon Sergeant K. called. They had tried the delivery but no one was home. I wanted to scream. The board users kept posting how the suspense was driving them nuts. Well, it was going to give me an aneurysm. A million possibilities went through my head. Maybe he had somebody working at FedEx who tipped him off? Maybe I worded something in one of my e-mails a little off? Sergeant K. called me back to let me know they would try the delivery again the next day. He also wanted to let me know that they had intercepted another package that was being sent to the same address. Looks like he'd already struck again! Thankfully, the lady from New York would get her computer back. He also told me that he was definitely going to keep pursuing this, and that, oddly enough, the address I'd given him was also related to another fraud case; this one much bigger (hundreds of thousands) and involving a certain Chicago franchise I won't mention. So maybe I had led them to something bigger than just another small-time counterfeiter.

I had finals all day. I'm a 4.0 honors student. I'd had a 4.0 all semester, but I wasn't sure I'd keep it after that day. I couldn't sleep the night before. All I could think about was Mr. Christmas and the delivery. I couldn't study either. So I winged it. I called Sergeant K. at 2:45. He told me he was on his way back to the house. They'd already made the delivery and arrested the guy. He had more than $10,000 in counterfeit cashier's checks waiting for deliveries.

When will criminals learn? You just shouldn't mess with Mac people! Here are the sites with great users that helped me out. You can sign up for the forums and read all about this as it was going on.

➤ www.macrumor.com

➤ www.macnn.com

➤ www.thinksecret.com

➤ www.powerpage.org

➤ www.whitepages.com

➤ www.fonefinder.com

➤ http://www.bethanyrayne.com/clcellmagic.htm

Figure 11.3 *Smith news article with picture*

Epilogue

Jason never did get his PowerBook back. But General Cybernetics, an Alabama-based Apple reseller, read about his misfortune and donated a brand new iBook to Smith. By busting the con man, Jason also got his 15 minutes of fame. His exploits appeared in newspapers around the globe, and Connie Chung interviewed him on CNN during Christmas week, 2002. Ironically, Jason didn't own a TV set on which to watch it. So he watched his world premiere sitting on a barstool in a local pub. I can't make up my mind which movie Smith's story reminds me of more, *The Sting* or *Rocky*. I guess it's the eBay version of *Rocky*.

Don't Get Mad. Get Even!

When Steve Kirsch, the Silicon Valley mogul who sued fax.com for $2.2 trillion (Chapter 5) read Smith's story, he paid him the ultimate compliment. He said, "This guy is as tenacious as I am!" Jason and Steve both illustrate that it doesn't take money to get even—it takes outrage and ingenuity! Because of what each accomplished, I dedicate this book to them and countless others like them, who have used technology to turn the tables on the technology that victimized them. Let them serve as your example. The next time you're targeted, victimized, or someone tries to invade your privacy, fight back! Turn the tables on whomever or whatever, and pull out the rug from under them!

PART II
Zone Defense

The Hacker's Guide To Privacy

We've come full circle. The first section of this book examined the dark side of technology; the final section reveals the bright side; how to use technology to protect your privacy. Figure II.1 pinpoints the zones in which our privacy is subject to invasion. Regardless of which zone you're in, there are practical steps you can take to secure your privacy and personal information. I sought the advice of several hackers and security experts profiled in this book to prepare a practical guide to help you protect yourself. That's what zone defense is all about.

You're a target! Wherever you go, there you are. Presence awareness technology is here. Our information is being harvested and there's nothing we can do about it! But you can protect your privacy by practicing stealth and using your digital doppelganger. Common sense and technological countermeasures can help you evade the invaders!

I hope you enjoyed reading this book as much as I enjoyed writing it. I'd like to end it with these three words...

Think for yourself!

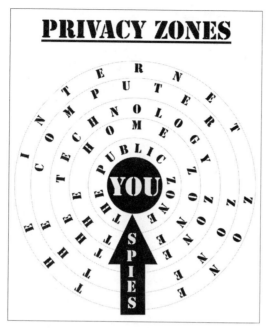

Figure II.1 *Privacy zones illustration*

Figure II.2 *Target illustration*

CHAPTER 12

The Computer Zone

- Creating a Dummy Administrator Account for Troubleshooting
- Passwords
- Convenience versus Paranoia
- Using a Good Antivirus Software
- Using a Good Firewall
- Password-Protecting Your Computer

A computer is an awesome tool, but in the wrong hands it can be turned into a weapon and used against you. Computers far more powerful than yours have been networked to harvest your data, observe your behavior, track your whereabouts, and note your demographic preferences. Securing your PC is the first step toward securing your privacy. The default settings on a new computer are aimed at the novice user and the lowest common denominator. They're notoriously insecure! If you haven't already tweaked your PC, isn't it about time?

Keep in mind that any computer setting that can be disabled can also be enabled, and vice versa! The perfect computer balances usability, stability, performance, and security. Before you customize your PC, answer these questions:

➤ What is your computer's primary use?

➤ Where is the computer located?

➤ How many people have access to the computer?

➤ Is the computer a server or on a network?

➤ Is the computer stationary or mobile?

➤ Who owns the computer?

➤ Is the computer for company or personal use?

➤ Could spyware or monitoring software already be installed on the machine?

➤ What is your computer's risk quotient on a scale of 1 to 10?

➤ What are the odds of your computer being compromised, hacked, or physically stolen?

Now follow these steps to set up your computer accordingly.

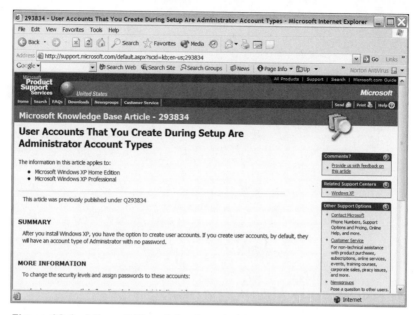

Figure 12.1 *Microsoft Knowledge Base Article 293834—User Accounts That You Create During Setup Are Administrator Account Types*

The Administrator Account

If you create additional user accounts after you install Windows XP, they'll be set up as administrator accounts with no passwords by default. When you set up multiple user accounts on one machine, any user with administrator access can view the documents in another user's My Documents folder, for example. If you're the computer administrator, here's how to plug this security hole.

1. Click User Accounts in the Category View Control Panel. If you favor the Classic View Control Panel, double-click.
2. Click Change an Account.
3. Click the user account that you want to modify.
4. Click Change the Account Type.
5. Select the desired account type for this user account.
6. Click the Change Account Type button.
7. To assign a password to this account, click Create a Password.

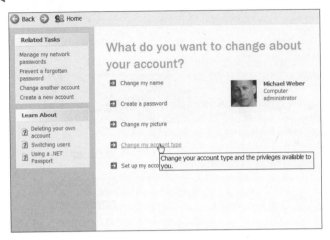

Figure 12.2 *User Account Controls*

Granting Other User Accounts Limited Access

To ensure the utmost security and privacy, if you're the computer administrator, grant limited status to other accounts and restrict user access by assigning each user an individual password.

If you have Windows XP formatted as NTFS, the native file format of Windows XP, NT, and 2000, you can also hide files and folders.

To protect a folder

1. Right-click the folder.
2. Select Properties.
3. Click the Sharing tab.
4. Select Make This Folder Private.

Windows XP will prompt you to create a password or risk subjecting your private information to public scrutiny. No one, not even fellow system administrators, can access the files once you make the folder private. Every file or folder contained within the folders you choose to make private will take on the settings of the parent folder.

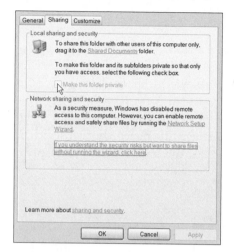

Figure 12.3 *Folder Properties privacy feature*

Creating a Dummy Administrator Account for Troubleshooting

Here's a tip I heard from Leo Laporte on TechTV's *The Screen Savers*.

Create an extra administrator account that you don't use on your Windows XP or Mac OS X machine. This dummy account will come in handy if you ever have trouble with your main account. If you can log in to your dummy account but not your main account, the problem is with the user-specific settings of your main account.

To create a dummy administrator account in Windows XP

1. Click User Accounts in the Control Panel.
2. Select Create a New Account.
3. Follow the steps in the wizard.
4. Select the Computer Administrator option and assign the account your normal password.

To create a dummy administrator account in Mac OS X

1. Open the Accounts System Preferences pane.
2. Click the New User button.
3. Assign the user the same password as your day-to-day account and enable administrator privileges for the new account.

Passwords

If your computer is sitting alone at home, chances are you don't need a password. If others have access to your PC or if it's mobile, you not only require a password, you also need a definitive password strategy. The object is to make it as difficult as possible for a cracker to guess your password. This leaves the cracker no alternative but to mount a brute-force search, trying every possible combination of letters, numbers, and punctuation. A search of this sort—even conducted on a machine that can compute one million passwords per second (most machines can compute less than one hundred per second)—would require more than a hundred years to complete.

Password don'ts:

> ➤ Don't use your login name in any form.
> ➤ Don't use your first or last name in any form.
> ➤ Don't use your spouse's, pet's, or child's name.
> ➤ Don't use license plate numbers, telephone numbers, social security numbers, the brand of your automobile, your street address, and so on.
> ➤ Don't use a password comprised of all digits or of all the same letter.
> ➤ Don't use words contained in English or foreign language dictionaries, spelling lists, and so on.
> ➤ Don't use a password that has fewer than six characters.

Password dos:

> ➤ Do use a password that will be easy to remember and that you don't have to write down.
> ➤ Do use a password with mixed-case alphabetic characters (uPAnDdOwN).
> ➤ Do use a password with non-alphabetic characters such as digits and punctuation (!q@W3#edc).
> ➤ Do use a password you can type quickly, without having to look at the keyboard. This will make it more difficult for someone to steal your password by spying.

How to choose a password that's easy to remember:

> Use the memorized street address of a distant friend or relative (7925mAiN).

> Choose a line from a song and use the first letter of each word. "He's a real nowhere man sitting in his nowhere land" becomes HarNmsiHNl, but it's easy to remember.

> Use two short words and concatenate them with a punctuation character in between, like the password on an AOL CD (dOg;raIn, Book+muG, kiD?Goat, and so on).

> Use your imagination. A good password pays dividends every time you use it, so creating one should be fun!

Windows System Restore

What good is a computer that won't boot? System Restore is among Windows' most valuable utilities. Microsoft enables it by default, but some manufacturers disable it to conserve disk space. Here's how you can determine whether System Restore is enabled and adjust its size.

1. Right-click on My Computer.

2. Select Properties.

3. Click the System Restore tab.

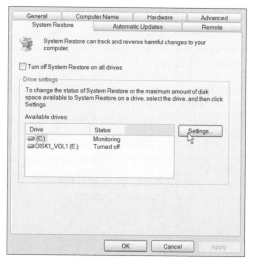

Figure 12.4 *System Restore utility size settings*

On hard drives larger that 4 GB, the default size of System Restore is approximately 12 percent of the logical drive on which Windows is installed. Microsoft hasn't changed this default since XP was launched, but hard drives have grown exponentially. Two gigabytes for System Restore is generally enough. Each restore point is approximately 50 MB. Forty restore points is plenty for average use. If you change your computer configuration quite often, reserve more disk space accordingly.

Get in the Habit of Creating Restore Points

Prior to installing any new applications or making any major changes to your system settings, create a restore point. Windows supposedly creates restore points every 24 hours, but I find it reassuring to create my own restore points manually. You should create a restore point now, before you make any of the changes I'm about to suggest. There are several ways to access System Restore:

> **Start menu**
> > Click Help and Support, Performance and Maintenance, Using System Restore to Undo Changes.
> > Click All Programs, Accessories, System Tools, System Restore.
> **Windows XP Control Panel (Category View)**. Click Performance and Maintenance and then select System Restore located in the left pane of the Control Panel under "See Also."

To create a restore point

1. Open System Restore.
2. Click Create a Restore Point.
3. Click Next.
4. Type an identifiable name (such as Before Invasion of Privacy Security Tweak) in the Restore Point Description field.
5. Click Create.
6. System Restore automatically adds the date and time to the name of your restore point.
7. Click Close.

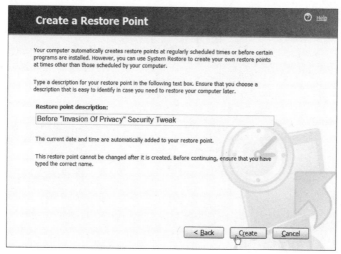

Figure 12.5 *Create a Restore Point screen*

Disabling Error Reporting

I find Microsoft's Error Reporting feature invasive and insulting. And as you can see from this bulletin posted on the U.S. Department of Energy CIAC (*Computer Incident Advisory Capability*) Web site, Error Reporting is also insecure.

DOE CIAC Warning

Office XP, Internet Explorer, and Windows XP use a feature called Error Reporting to send crash and debug information back to Microsoft to help them detect and fix bugs in their software. Unfortunately, Error Reporting can send portions of the document or Web site you are viewing along with this debugging information. The debugging information includes a memory dump which may contain all or part of the document being viewed or edited. This debug message potentially could contain sensitive, private information.

The last thing I want to see when a Windows program crashes is a dialog box from Microsoft rubbing it in my face. Sending Microsoft an Error Report takes time, drains my system, tries my patience, and transmits data I could regret transmitting. Disabling Error Reporting is now a simple affair, but prior to the latest XP/Office Service Packs, it required a registry hack, which really ticked me off! There is no reason to feel guilty either. According to Microsoft, more than 90 percent of these Error Reports pertain to fewer than 2 percent of all software bugs.

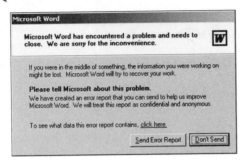

Figure 12.6 *Microsoft Error Reporting dialog box*

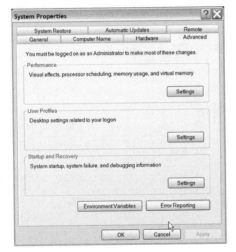

Figure 12.7 *Error Reporting button in System Properties*

To disable error reporting

1. Right-click My Computer.
2. Select Properties.
3. Click the Advanced tab in System Properties.
4. Click the Error Reporting button.
5. The Error Reporting dialog box will appear. Select Disable Error Reporting.

Figure 12.8 *Check Disable Error Reporting in the Error Reporting dialog box*

Disabling File and Printer Sharing

Unless you want to give a malicious hacker or corporation complete read/write access to the contents of your hard drive, disable file and printer sharing except when absolutely necessary. File and printer sharing leave your computer open to attack.

To disable Windows file sharing

1. Double-click My Computer.
2. Right-click each drive under Hard Disk Drives.
3. Select Properties.
4. Click the Sharing tab.
5. Ascertain that file sharing is disabled.

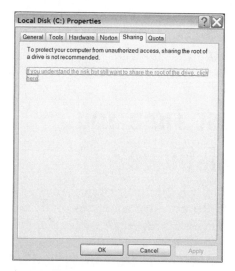

Figure 12.9 *File Sharing tab under Disk Properties*

Microsoft makes you jump through another hoop to disable file and printing sharing over the Internet. This redundancy is not only confusing, it's the worst kind of security breach—a blind spot! It's about time Microsoft got into the habit of placing redundant tasks like this on the same tab, don't you think?

To disable Internet file and printer sharing:

1. Open the Control Panel.
2. Click Network and Internet Connections.
4. Right-click each network connection.
5. Select Properties.
6. Uncheck File and Printer Sharing for Microsoft Networks on the Connection Properties page

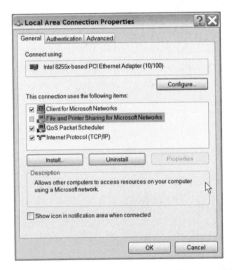

Figure 12.10 *Uncheck Disable Internet File and Printer Sharing for Microsoft Networks in the Connection Properties box*

When Was the Last Time You Used Remote Assistance?

The deeper I delve into Windows security holes, the more clueless Microsoft seems. An arcane feature in XP called Remote Assistance gives control of your PC to another user on a remote computer. Don't get me wrong; this feature is a useful tech tool. The problem is that it's woefully undocumented. And Microsoft enables it by default! It resides on the Remote tab in System Properties.

To disable Remote Assistance

1. Right-click My Computer.
2. Select Properties.
3. Click the Remote tab.
4. Uncheck Allow Remote Assistance Invitations to be Sent from This Computer.

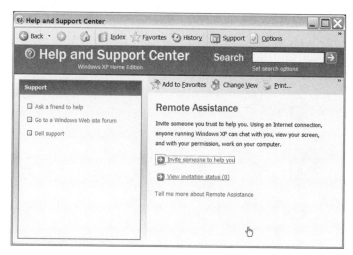

Figure 12.11 *Help and support about Remote Assistance*

Figure 12.12 *System Properties Remote tab*

Convenience versus Paranoia

Windows offers a plethora of convenient features. The Start menu remembers your most recently accessed files and programs, the Recycle Bin remembers what you've deleted, and Internet Explorer logs a history of each Web site you visit and fills in your passwords and personal information automatically. I admit it; as lazy as I am, I use most of these features. However, I'm the only user of my particular computer. The question is, do you want to leave a trail of where you've been and what you've been doing on the computer you're using?

Figure 12.13 *The Taskbar and Start Menu Properties dialog box*

To clear recent programs and documents from the Start menu

1. Right-click the Start menu.

2. Select Properties.

3. Click the Start Menu tab.

4. Click the Customize button.

5. On the General tab, enter 0 under Number of Programs on Start Menu.

6. Click the Clear List button.

7. On the Advanced tab, uncheck List My Most Recently Opened Documents.

8. Click the Clear List button.

Figure 12.14 *The Customize Start Menu tabs*

Tweak UI

Microsoft offers a convenient tool called Tweak UI with a so-called "paranoia" feature. You can download it and other free Windows XP PowerToys at http://www.microsoft.com/windowsxp/pro/downloads/powertoys.asp. If you don't want prying eyes to see what files you've been accessing, Tweak UI offers an option to clear your document history automatically each time you exit Windows.

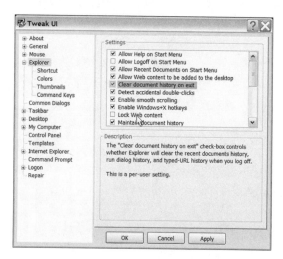

Figure 12.15 *Tweak UI Explorer settings*

To clear your document history automatically with Tweak UI

1. Open Tweak UI.
2. Click Explorer.
3. Under Settings, check Clear Document History on Exit.
4. Uncheck Maintain Document History.
5. Uncheck Maintain Network History.

The Recycle Bin

When you delete a file or document in Windows, it is sent to the Recycle Bin, but the file isn't deleted from your hard disk. This safeguards you from purging an important file from your system by mistake. But do you want prying eyes observing what files you've deleted?

To circumvent the Recycle Bin and delete a file permanently

1. Select the file in Windows Explorer.
2. Press Shift and Delete on your keyboard simultaneously.

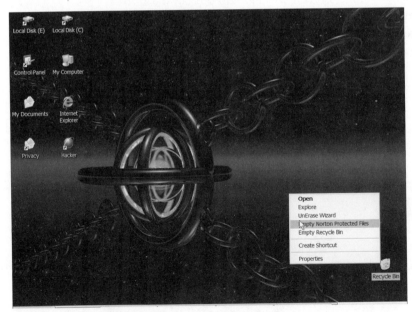

Figure 12.16 *The Recycle Bin pop-up menu*

To empty the Recycle Bin

1. Right-click the Recycle Bin.

2. Choose Empty Recycle Bin from the menu that appears.

As with System Restore, Microsoft has failed to adjust the Recycle Bin's default capacity to keep up with the capacity of today's huge hard drives. By default, it's set to one-tenth of the size of each hard disk, which could leave gigabytes of unwanted clutter to slow down your system. How large should the Recycle Bin cache be? Between 0 and 500 MB, depending on your ideal safety net and security needs. The lower the better! The maximum sizes of my Recycle Bins average between 300 and 400 MB each.

To adjust the capacity of the Recycle Bin

1. Right-click the Recycle Bin.

2. Select Properties.

3. On the Global tab, click Configure Drives Independently.

4. Select the tab for each drive and configure it accordingly

5. On the drive tab move the percentage slider so that "Space Reserved" reads around 400 MB.

6. Repeat for each hard drive.

To disable the Recycle Bin and delete files permanently

1. Right-click the Recycle Bin.

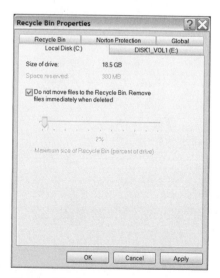

Figure 12.17 *The Recycle Bin Properties drive tab*

2. Select Properties.

2. Click the tab for each disk drive.

3. Check the Do Not Move Files to the Recycle Bin. Remove Files Immediately When Deleted option (also available on the Global tab).

Performing Disk Cleanup

I find the most convenient way to empty the Recycle Bin and delete other unnecessary cache files that leave a digital trail is to use the Windows Disk Cleanup utility.

To use Disk Cleanup

1. Double-click My Computer.

2. Right-click on a hard disk drive.

3. Select Properties.

4. Click the Disk Cleanup button on the General tab.

Caution

Do not check Compress Drive or Allow Indexing Services. They elongate disk cleaning and bog down the OS.

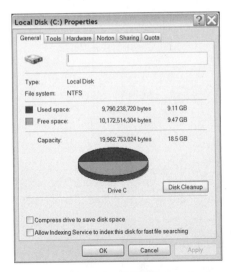

Figure 12.18 *The Disk Cleanup button*

Defragmenting Your Hard Drive

Even after you empty the Recycle Bin and permanently delete files, remnants of those files remain in empty sectors on your hard drive. With readily available forensic software, these files are easily recoverable. The simplest way to obliterate deleted file remnants from unused sectors is to defragment your hard drive regularly. Defragging is also a great way to boost system performance! The Windows Disk Defragment option is located on the Tools tab of the Properties page for each drive in My Computer.

Figure 12.19 *The Defragment Now button on the Disk Properties Tools tab*

Windows XP Professional Encryption

File encryption converts data into a format that others can't read. The Windows XP EFS (*Encrypting File System*) stores files in an encrypted format on your hard disk. Unfortunately, EFS isn't included in Microsoft Windows XP Home Edition.

To encrypt a file or folder in Windows XP professional

1. Start Windows Explorer.
2. Locate the file or folder you want to encrypt.

3. Right-click the file.

4. Click Properties.

5. On the General tab, click Advanced.

6. Under Compress or Encrypt Attributes, select the Encrypt Contents to Secure Data check box.

7. Click OK.

Figure 12.20 *Select Encrypt Contents to Secure Data in the Advanced Attributes dialog box*

If the file is located in an unencrypted folder, you will see an Encryption Warning dialog box.

If you want to encrypt only the file, click Encrypt the File Only, and then click OK. If you want to encrypt the file and the folder in which it is located, click Encrypt the File and the Parent Folder, and then click OK.

To encrypt a file in Microsoft Office XP

1. Click the Tools menu in the document you want to encrypt.

2. Select Options.

3. Click the Security tab.

4. Click Advanced under File Encryption Options for This Document.

5. Select an encryption method. (Remember that longer keys provide greater security.)

6. Click OK.

7. Enter a password.

8. Click OK.

You might not use file encryption on a regular basis, but it's good to know how to use it for truly sensitive documents.

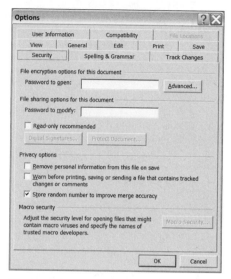

Figure 12.21 *The Office XP Tools Security tab*

Windows Update

Microsoft finds flaws and security holes in their products on a daily basis. The good news is that they acknowledge and patch them as fast as possible. If it's Wednesday it's Windows security patch day is the new tune at Microsoft! It is vital that you use Windows Update on a regular basis to keep ahead of the curve. Install all critical updates and security patches. You need to be online to access Windows Update.

To program Windows Update automatically

1. Open the Control Panel.
2. Click System under Performance and Maintenance.
3. Click the Automatic Updates tab.
4. Check Keep My Computer Up to Date.
5. Under Notification Settings, check the middle button—Download the updates automatically and notify me when they're ready to install.
6. Click Apply.

To access Windows update manually

1. Click the Start menu.
2. Select All Programs.
3. Select Windows Update.

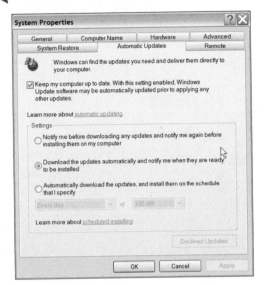

Figure 12.22 *The System Properties Automatic Updates tab*

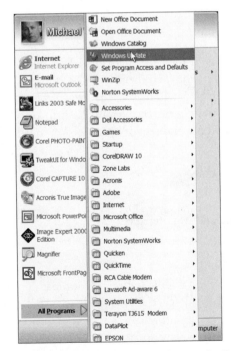

Figure 12.23 *Windows Update on the Start menu*

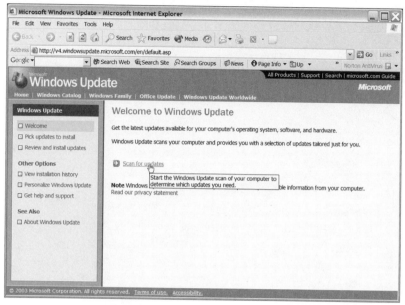

Figure 12.24 *The Windows Update site*

There are three tools without which no modern computer is secure:

➢ A good spyware scanner

➢ A good antivirus program

➢ A good personal firewall

Scanning for Spyware

It's wise to check your computer manufacturer's Web site for custom drivers before installing generic ones. Install XP components with great caution. Some third-party components contain the worst kind of spyware! WildTangent's 3D Visualization, a plug-in for Windows Media Player, is a good case in point. It installed 68 separate spyware components on my system, including registry entries, tracking software, folders, files, and cookies.

If a suspicious screen about sending information to WildTangent about their Web Driver hadn't raised the hackles on my neck during installation, WildTangent could be spying on me right now! A quick Google search for the keywords "WildTangent - spyware" confirmed my worst fear. WildTangent is spyware that craps up your system big time! I took a deep breath and let Ad-aware 6 do the rest. (You can go to http://www.lavasoft.de/software/

How to Hose Your Computer System in One Easy Click!

68 WildTangent Spyware Components

```
obj[1]=RegKey : CLSID\{083863F1-70DE-11d0-BD40-00A0C911CE86}\Instance\
               {ECFBE6E0-1AC8-11D4-8501-00A0CC5D1F63}
obj[2]=RegKey : CLSID\{7F23E6E5-0E79-4aee-B723-B1463805D5A9}
obj[3]=RegKey : CLSID\{8ECF83A0-1AC9-11D4-8501-00A0CC5D1F63}
obj[4]=RegKey : CLSID\{AB29A544-D6B4-4E36-A1F8-D3E34FC7B00A}
obj[5]=RegKey : CLSID\{B9BA256A-075B-49ea-B9E2-7DBC2EF021D5}
obj[6]=RegKey : CLSID\{ECFBE6E0-1AC8-11D4-8501-00A0CC5D1F63}
obj[7]=RegKey : CLSID\{FA13A9FA-CA9B-11D2-9780-00104B242EA3}
obj[8]=RegKey : Interface\{05EF74A5-E109-11D2-A566-444553540000}
obj[9]=RegKey : Interface\{0E7AE465-EE8D-11D2-A566-444553540000}
obj[10]=RegKey : Interface\{1113C0B6-5300-4D5D-B2D7-35C14B28341B}
obj[11]=RegKey : Interface\{111D8B01-96C5-46DD-94D1-C6E8B1F69F44}
obj[12]=RegKey : Interface\{16410859-886F-4579-BC1F-330A139D0F0F}
obj[13]=RegKey : Interface\{35ED7DFB-A8ED-4216-A4BB-BC08C326EF08}
obj[14]=RegKey : Interface\{3F44B498-8FD4-4A1E-852C-170156ED27C0}
obj[15]=RegKey : Interface\{52889E01-CB46-11D2-96BC-00104B242E64}
obj[16]=RegKey : Interface\{5C49CBD2-8ED7-439B-8668-32149F84A235}
obj[17]=RegKey : Interface\{6E6CF8E5-D795-11D2-A566-444553540000}
obj[18]=RegKey : Interface\{79884200-3ADE-11D3-AC39-00105A2057FA}
obj[19]=RegKey : Interface\{AA0C96F9-A994-42D7-9543-842CF85E1BA7}
obj[20]=RegKey : Interface\{B57613B6-EF02-4D96-99C6-70C9A2014A14}
obj[21]=RegKey : Interface\{BDB9B021-CAFF-11D2-9780-00104B242EA3}
obj[22]=RegKey : Interface\{BDB9B022-CAFF-11D2-9780-00104B242EA3}
obj[23]=RegKey : Interface\{D72AC8E7-F41D-11D2-A566-444553540000}
obj[24]=RegKey : Interface\{DE3E540A-F0F2-4761-99BE-AFC6DC427E30}
obj[25]=RegKey : Interface\{EA6F254D-1A8C-4518-8FE0-E9B94FD134ED}
obj[26]=RegKey : Interface\{EC914A5C-7C4B-4AC8-8C86-C10FF5C0D23D}
obj[27]=RegKey : Interface\{F10493C1-D0B6-11D2-A566-444553540000}
obj[28]=RegKey : Interface\{FA13AA3A-CA9B-11D2-9780-00104B242EA3}
obj[29]=RegKey : Interface\{FA13AA3E-CA9B-11D2-9780-00104B242EA3}
obj[30]=RegKey : Interface\{FA13AA40-CA9B-11D2-9780-00104B242EA3}
obj[31]=RegKey : Interface\{FA13AA44-CA9B-11D2-9780-00104B242EA3}
obj[32]=RegKey : Interface\{FA13AA46-CA9B-11D2-9780-00104B242EA3}
obj[33]=RegKey : Interface\{FA13AA50-CA9B-11D2-9780-00104B242EA3}
obj[34]=RegKey : Interface\{FA13AAFA-CA9B-11D2-9780-00104B242EA3}
```

```
obj[35]=RegKey : SOFTWARE\Microsoft\Windows\CurrentVersion\Uninstall\wcmd-
                 mgr.exe
obj[36]=RegKey : SOFTWARE\Microsoft\Windows\CurrentVersion\Uninstall\wtweb-
                 driver
obj[37]=RegKey : SOFTWARE\WildTangent
obj[38]=RegKey : TypeLib\{B7E20302-C22C-4AF2-9D75-C3EB6EEE9DD8}
obj[39]=RegKey : TypeLib\{FA13AA2E-CA9B-11D2-9780-00104B242EA3}
obj[40]=RegKey : WDMHHost.WTHoster
obj[41]=RegKey : WDMHHost.WTHoster.1
obj[42]=RegKey : WT3D.WT
obj[43]=RegKey : WT3D.WT.1
obj[44]=RegKey : WTVis.WTVisReceiver
obj[45]=RegKey : WTVis.WTVisReceiver.1
obj[46]=RegKey : WTVis.WTVisSender
obj[47]=RegKey : WTVis.WTVisSender.1
obj[48]=RegValue : Control Panel\MMCPL
obj[49]=RegValue : SOFTWARE\Microsoft\Windows\CurrentVersion\Run
obj[50]=RegValue : Software\Microsoft\Windows\CurrentVersion\Run
obj[51]=Folder : C:\Program Files\Windows Media Player\Visualizations\
                 wtupdates
obj[52]=Folder : C:\WINDOWS\wt\wtupdates\wtupdater
obj[53]=Folder : C:\WINDOWS\wt\wtupdates\wtwebdriver
obj[54]=Folder : C:\WINDOWS\wt\wtupdates
obj[56]=File : c:\windows\wt\backup\1.5.1.36\stopwcmdr.bat
obj[57]=File : c:\windows\wt\backup\1.5.1.36\updatenow.bat
obj[58]=File : c:\windows\wt\backup\1.5.1.36\wcmdmgr.exe
obj[59]=File : c:\windows\wt\backup\1.5.1.36\wcmdmgr1.exe
obj[60]=File : c:\windows\wt\updater\stopwcmdr.bat
obj[61]=File : c:\windows\wt\updater\updatenow.bat
obj[62]=File : c:\windows\wt\updater\wcmdmgr1.exe
obj[63]=File : c:\windows\wt\updater\wt.ini
obj[64]=File : c:\windows\wt\wtupdates\wtwebdriver\files\2.1.1.045\legacy\
               webdriver.dll
obj[65]=File : c:\windows\wt\wtupdates\wtwebdriver\files\2.1.1.045\legacy\
               wt3d.dll
obj[66]=File : c:\windows\wt\webdriver.dll
obj[67]=File : c:\windows\wt\wt3d.dll
obj[68]=File : c:\windows\wt\wt3d.ini
```

adaware to download Ad-aware or visit the *Invasion of Privacy* homepage at http://www.mjweber.com/iop/privacy.htm) I'm pleased to report that Microsoft has removed all links to WildTangent plug-ins from its Media Player Web site.

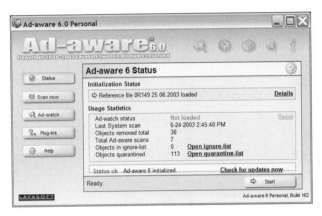

Figure 12.25 *Ad-aware 6 spyware scan*

Ad-aware was going bonkers. I never saw so many hits in a single scan! I quarantined the spyware components and then deleted WildTangent using Add or Remove Programs in Control Panel. I should have quit when I was ahead! Plagued by the notion that some WildTangent components had eluded Ad-aware, I decided to do a System Restore prior to the date of the WildTangent install.

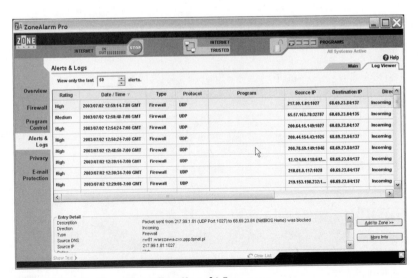

Figure 12.26 *ZoneAlarm Pro Alerts & Logs page*

That's when my trouble really began! I had just updated ZoneAlarm Pro, my personal firewall. After the System Restore, ZoneAlarm's product version clashed with its security engine version, and I had to uninstall, reinstall and reconfigure ZoneAlarm. All of this grief because I inadvertently installed this scummy spyware! Unfortunately, there's no way to avoid my fate. Software makers and marketers have entered into an unholy alliance to invade our privacy. Refer to the list of WildTangent's corporate partners in Chapter 9 to get a picture of who's spying on you. Your only recourse is to possess the tools to undo the damage done by spyware and to use them. That's the trick!

Using a Good Antivirus Software

If your system doesn't have antivirus protection like Norton or McAfee, install it immediately! Sooner or later a virus or worm will compromise your computer. An antivirus program can circumvent that and prevent a real calamity.

You'll find links to download numerous utilities including antivirus, anti-spyware, and personal firewalls on the *Invasion of Privacy* homepage at http://www.mjweber.com/iop/privacy.htm/.

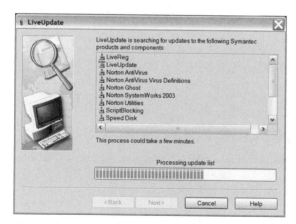

Figure 12.27 *Norton AntiVirus LiveUpdate*

Updating Your Virus Definitions

Don't be penny-wise and pound-foolish. It's important to keep your antivirus library up to date. An antivirus subscription runs about $15 a year. Open your wallet—but check eBay first. You might be able to upgrade the product version of your favorite antivirus program, including a one-year subscription, for the same investment. Last July I bought the latest version of Norton Systemworks Pro, a great suite of utilities that includes Norton AntiVirus, for $11 on eBay. Once an *Internet Auction Junkie*, always an internet auction junkie!

Once you have a valid subscription, use it weekly to update your virus definitions. Most antivirus programs have an auto-update feature, but I prefer to update mine manually. I favor minimizing the number of Windows services running in the background of my system.

Antivirus programs have two modes:

> ➤ **Set it and forget it**. (The program starts automatically upon boot.)
> ➤ **Scan for viruses**. (The program allows on-demand scanning of files, folders, or the complete computer system.)

Scanning for Viruses

In addition to the "set it and forget it" mode, it's prudent to do a full virus scan of your computer system weekly.

Reserve an hour per week to

> ➤ Defrag your hard drive. (Remember to perform a Disk Cleanup first.)
> ➤ Update your virus definitions.
> ➤ Scan your computer system for viruses.
> ➤ Scan your computer system for spyware.

Performing On-Demand Virus Scans

It's also wise to scan shareware and third-party downloads for viruses prior to and after installation. I use Norton, but all antivirus programs have similar feature sets.

To scan files or folders for viruses on demand with Norton

1. Open Windows Explorer.
2. Click the Folders button on the navigation bar if you don't see a directory tree in the left pane.
3. Right-click any file or folder.
4. Choose Scan with (Norton) AntiVirus.

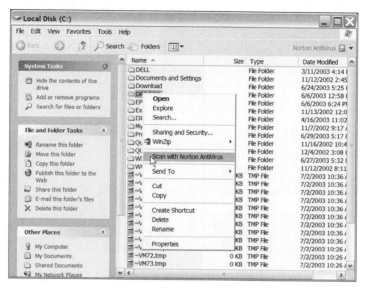

Figure 12.28 *Windows Explorer Scan with Norton AntiVirus option*

Using a Good Firewall

Firewalls gobble up precious system resources, especially on older computers and operating systems, so I wouldn't recommend one if it wasn't a necessity. Once upon a time, there was a debate over whether a firewall was necessary if you connected to the Internet using a dial-up connection. However, crackers and data thieves randomly barrage PCs connected to the Internet with pings and port scans, probing for unprotected systems. Once such a system is found, a cracker can compromise it with a Trojan horse, spyware, or a malicious worm. The bottom line is that any personal computer connected to the Internet is a potential target. My computer, with its broadband connection, is accessed hundreds of times a day by hackers, spies, and corporate snoops probing my computer for vulnerabilities. Each alert in the ZoneAlarm log shown in Figure 12.26 is an example of an unwelcome intruder!

Even if you only use a dial-up connection an hour a day, your computer is vulnerable. Your only viable option is to use a firewall for protection. Windows XP comes with a built-in bare-bones firewall, but I don't recommend it. I suggest you install the free version of ZoneAlarm instead. I use ZoneAlarm Pro, which also blocks cookies and pop-up ads. I consider it the most bulletproof firewall available. Follow the prompts to download a free version at http://www.zonelabs.com.

> **Note**
> Be sure to disable XP's built-in firewall prior to installing ZoneAlarm.

To disable Windows XP's built-in firewall

1. Open the Control Panel.
2. Click on Network and Internet Connections
2. Click on Network Connections.
3. Right-click on each Internet connection (including dial-up, LAN, or high-speed).
4. Select Properties.
5. Click the Advanced tab.
6. Uncheck the box in the Internet Connection Firewall section.

Unlike an antivirus or spyware detection, which must be activated to scan your system, a firewall is pretty much "set it and forget it." Once installed, the firewall keeps your personal data and privacy safe from hackers and data thieves, and protects your PC from intrusion and attack. By blocking the ports of your computer, a firewall makes your machine invisible to other computers on the Internet. If you can't be seen, you can't be attacked! That's the principle behind practicing stealth (Chapter 3).

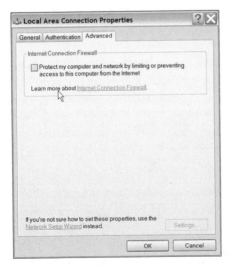

Figure 12.29 *The Internet Connection Firewall dialog box*

Software Defaults

An old truism states that a computer is only as good as the applications installed on its hard drive. The new truism is software manufacturers take a lot of liberties when it comes to collecting information about us. They do this by soliciting our implicit permission to harvest information in their software defaults.

When you install an application, read each screen carefully and opt out of any and all data harvesting options. When in doubt, leave it out! No software developer, large or small, is above data harvesting. Following are a few examples.

Windows Media Player 9

Windows Media Player 9 offers better privacy control to consumers than its predecessor did. In prior versions, you had to hack Windows Registry to prevent Media Player from sending a unique player ID to content providers and usage data back to Microsoft. Media Player 9 makes it easier to disable these features, but it still, by default, keeps track of private files and Web-based content that you access.

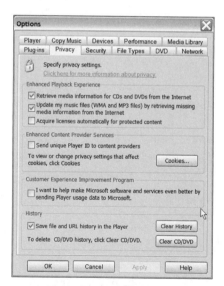

Figure 12.30 *The Windows Media Player 9 Privacy tab*

To control privacy settings in Windows Media Player 9:

1. Open Windows Media Player 9.
2. Click the Tools menu.
3. Click Options.
4. Click the Privacy tab.
5. Check Retrieve Media Information for CDs and DVDs from the Internet.
6. Check Update My Media Files by Retrieving Missing Media Information from the Internet.
7. Uncheck everything else on the Privacy tab. (You can leave History checked if you elect to maintain a history.)

Windows Media Player gets better with each version, but it's a crippled product at best. To unleash its full power, you must spend extra money on plugins for features that are free in rival players such as MusicMatch and WinAmp. Although Microsoft removed WildTangent's spyware from its Web site, it was a featured plug-in for Media Player 9 when I downloaded it. By the time Microsoft pulled it, the damage was already done! Then there's Digital Rights Management, the direction Microsoft seems to be boring full steam ahead. Quite frankly, I don't trust Windows Media Player for that reason, and I rarely use it; I use MusicMatch Jukebox instead.

MusicMatch Jukebox

MusicMatch is in the business of producing the best media player. They have no interest in controlling Digital Rights Management for media conglomerates and cutting themselves in on a share of the profits like Microsoft has. MusicMatch is not without privacy issues, however. During installation MusicMatch recommends that you "upload user preference data based on your user profile," by default. I suggest you don't.

To check whether you're being profiled by MusicMatch

1. Open MusicMatch Jukebox.
2. Click the Options menu.
3. Click Settings.
4. Uncheck the Upload User Preference Information Based on Listening Profile option under Permission to Communicate with MusicMatch Server on the General tab.

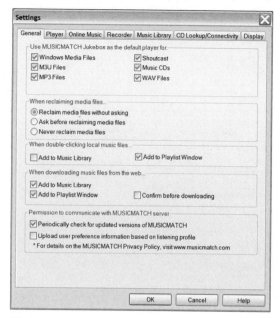

Figure 12.31 *The MusicMatch Settings with the Permission to Communicate with MusicMatch Server check boxes*

The Google Toolbar

I couldn't live without the Google toolbar! As a researcher, writer, general know-it-all, the Google toolbar makes me complete. Yet it also has privacy issues. If you elect to use the advanced features of the Google toolbar, such as the page rank feature, information about the sites you visit will be sent to Google by default. However, this advanced functionality is optional, and you can easily disable it.

To disable Google toolbar Web site tracking

1. Click Google on the Google toolbar.

2. Select Privacy Information.

3. Click the Disable All Advanced Features button.

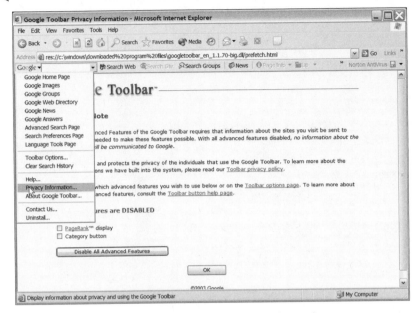

Figure 12.32 *The Google toolbar Privacy Information option*

It's Safe to Assume That All Software Profiles and Tracks You!

The Google toolbar, MusicMatch Jukebox, and Windows Media Player are merely examples. If you own software that doesn't spy on you, it's the exception rather than the rule. The onus is on you to examine the default settings of your software and the privacy policies of the Web sites you access. It's also your responsibility to opt out of all information exchange except that which is absolutely necessary to use a product or service!

Don't Ask, Don't Tell

If you don't ask how your privacy is being invaded, they won't tell you!

Out-of-the-Box Defaults

Out of the box, most new computers come with software defaults that bog down the system and could potentially invade your privacy! The fewer tasks, services, and processes that execute at startup, the faster your system will boot and run. Look at your Taskbar icon tray and answer this question: do you really need to have all those programs running, or could you live without some? Take back control of your PC! Disable all tasks services, and processes that aren't essential.

Essential boot-up processes:

> Antivirus

> Firewall

> Windows system controls

> Peripheral and application drivers

> Options you can't live without

I disabled 16 out of 22 tasks programmed to launch when my PC boots. As a lefty, I can't live without a little application called SwitchMouse-Buttons.exe. Adaptec installs a DirectCD driver because I burn CD-RWs. Norton is my antivirus, ZoneAlarm Pro is my firewall, wfxsnt40 is my WinFax driver, and Rundll32 initializes NVIDIA's display panel. Those are the only tasks I allow to start at boot-up!

Optimizing Your Startup

Before you optimize your computer's startup sequence, go to http://www.answersthatwork.com. This valuable site has a definitive list of Windows startup services, and it provides expert advice on those you can and can't live without. Click the Library of Answers That Work button. On the next page, click The TASK LIST. Now open Windows System Configuration utility.

To open the System Configuration utility

1. Click the Start menu.

2. Click Run.

3. In the Run box, type **msconfig**.

4. Click OK, and the System Configuration Utility will open.

5. Click the Startup tab.

6. Refer to each startup item on the Library of Answers That Work Web site. Click the letter of the alphabet that correspond to your startup items.

7 Uncheck all unnecessary startup items.

8. Click Apply.

9. Reboot your computer.

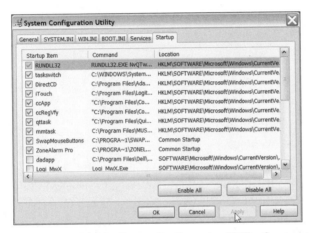

Figure 12.33 *The System Configuration Utility Startup tab*

When your computer reboots, a message will inform you that you have booted using Selective Startup. Click the Do Not Display This Message Again check box.

Password-Protecting Your Computer

It's prudent to password-protect your user account, especially if you have private or confidential documents that you don't want other users to access. It's also essential to password-protect a laptop computer if you travel with one. To create an effective password, refer to the advice in the "Passwords" section earlier in this chapter.

To password-protect your user account

1. Open the Control Panel.
2. Click User Accounts.
3. Click Change an Account.
4. Select your user account.
5. Click Create a Password.
6. Type in the new password.
7. Confirm the new password by typing it in a second time.
8. Create a password hint.
9. Click Create Password.

There's no easy way to access Windows XP if you forget a password. To prevent being locked out if you forget your password, create a password reset disk:

1. Insert a blank floppy disk into your floppy drive.
2. Open User Accounts in the Control Panel.
3. Click on your account name.
4. On the left side of the window, under Related Tasks, select Prevent a Forgotten Password.

A wizard will walk you through the process of creating a password recovery disk.

CHAPTER 13
The Internet Zone

- ➤ Opt-Out Sites
- ➤ The Cookie Monster
- ➤ Web Bugs
- ➤ The First Step to Protect Yourself on the Internet
- ➤ E-Mail and Its Evil Twin

The Web site http://www.digicrime.com hijacks your Web browser, alters the appearance of your computer desktop, warns you that your identity has been compromised, and triggers an alert from your antivirus program that you have an infection. The people behind DigiCrime claim their Web site is harmless and they're simply out to prove a point—how vulnerable the average computer system and Web browser actually are. These guys might be white hat hackers, but I don't find their "tough love" approach funny, even though they claim it's a joke. Even if this prank doesn't cause any long-term damage, it could crash your system and lose any unsaved work, not to mention give you a panic attack. I surf the Web for a living, and I must admit that certain Web sites make me feel like taking a shower after I visit them!

The Internet has some very bad neighborhoods, and if you don't know how to defend yourself, you could be hacked, cracked, and attacked! Fraud, spam, crime, and terrorism flourish on the Web because the Internet is the ultimate democracy. Even after 9/11, laws are impossible to enforce because ones like

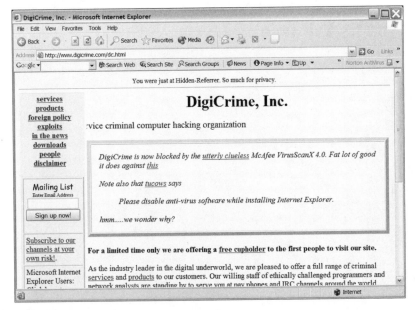

Figure 13.1 *The DigiCrime.com Web site*

The USA Patriot Act are designed to protect the homeland, not the consumer. Laws like The USA Patriot Act could even have inadvertent consequences, like enabling the government to spy on consumers. The jury is still out on that question because Congress has yet to enact effective laws to protect consumers on the Internet like the national "do not call" list protects them against telemarketers. Until such legislation is passed, it's up to each and every one of us to protect ourselves!

> **Note**
>
> Remember: Enable your firewall and antivirus before surfing the Web!

Opt-Out Sites

The Center for Democracy & Technology (http://opt-out.cdt.org/featured) has a great site that enables you to opt out of 14 major Web portals and online profilers (MSN, Wired, Yahoo, American Express, Any Birthday, AT&T, eBay, Amazon, 24/7 Media, AvenueA, BeFree, CoreMetrics, DoubleClick, and MediaPlex) in about twice as many mouse clicks. The site also offers savvy advice about online privacy.

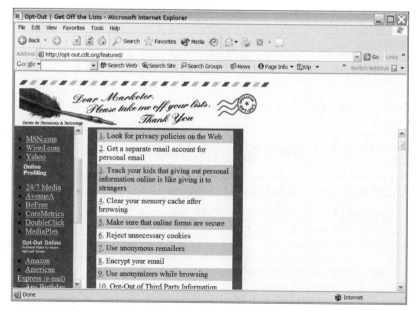

Figure 13.2 *The CDT Opt-Out site*

The Federal Trade Commission National "Do Not Call" Registry

The FTC's national "do not call" registry is now up and running. After opting out on the CDT site, I suggest you navigate to the FTC site at http://www.ftc.gov/bcp/conline/edcams/donotcall/index.html and opt out of telemarketing calls and junk faxes. Links to both sites are on the *Invasion of Privacy* homepage at http://www.mjweber.com/iop/privacy.htm.

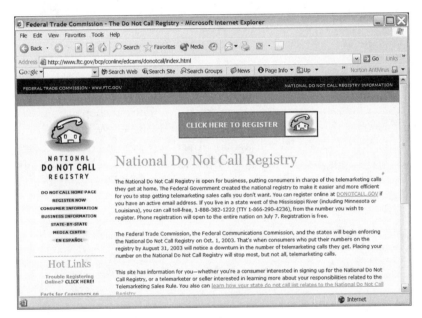

Figure 13.3 *The FTC "do not call" registry*

Don't Fall for Strong-Arm Tactics

Just because a Web site insists that you register doesn't mean you have to tell them your life story. You don't have to tell them anything! I often submit a bogus name and e-mail address to insistent Web sites that I visit only occasionally. The three most effective techniques for protecting your privacy apply universally.

> ➤ When in doubt, leave it out!

> ➤ Practice stealth!

> ➤ Use your digital doppelganger!

Beware of Web Sites with No User Agreement

Web sites that ask you to provide even innocuous information can learn a lot about you by connecting your browsing habits to your data. They can decipher the sites you visit, the type of computer you use, and what your interests are. Never register with a Web site that doesn't have a user agreement or a privacy policy.

Opt Out When You Register

Registering with certain Web sites, such as eBay, provides a real benefit. But it's up to you to track down their privacy policies for instruction on how to opt out of all nonessential contact, information exchange, and third-party information sharing. Don't leave this until later—opt out now!

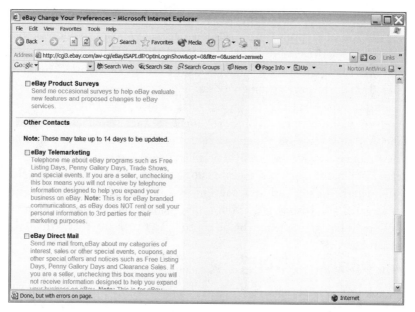

Figure 13.4 *eBay opt-out options*

Transactional Passwords versus Convenience

When it comes to registering with a site with which you intend to conduct business, such as a banking site, Amazon, or UPS, remember to employ secure password basics. However, many sites require a different password approach—convenience! I want instant access to sites with which I don't exchange confidential information, such as newspapers, downloads, and gaming. When it comes to registering with convenience sites, I use the same user name and password across the board. It's simple to remember, such as user name "john," password "lennon" or user name "miami," password "vice." That way I don't have to think twice to log on.

The Cookie Monster

Lou Montulli was the ninth employee hired by Netscape. In June 1994, the 24-year-old computer programmer sat down at his keyboard to address one of the biggest issues facing the fledgling World Wide Web—finding a way for Web sites to recognize users who had visited the site previously. Montulli hammered out a five-page document describing a technology that would revolutionize the Web by giving it a memory. He named his technology "cookies," and the rest is history! Cookies are small ID files stored on your hard drive by Web sites you visit. When you return to the site, the server connects your new request to your previous ID number, giving the company an ongoing record of what you view on the site. Not all cookies are bad. Within certain parameters, cookies can be a convenience, but many sites use them to deliver targeted advertising, track your online habits, and profile you. Internet Explorer 6 has rudimentary cookie control. To tweak Internet Explorer's cookie settings:

1. Click Tools on Internet Explorer's menu bar.
2. Click Internet Options.
3. Click the Privacy tab.
4. Click the Advanced button.
5. Check Override Automatic Cookie Handling.
6. Check Accept under First-Party Cookies.
7. Check Block under Third-Party Cookies.

Figure 13.5 *Internet Options—Advanced Privacy Settings*

8. Uncheck Always Allow Session Cookies.

9. Click OK or Apply.

Install a Cookie Manager

In addition to customizing Internet Explorer's privacy settings, I use the built-in privacy features in ZoneAlarm Pro to manage cookies. If you desire further control over cookies, http://www.cookiecentral.com is a good site for downloading freeware, shareware, and commercial cookie managers.

To delete cookies in Internet Explorer 6

1. Click Tools on Internet Explorer's menu bar.

2. Click Internet Options.

3. Click the Delete Cookies button under Temporary Internet Files.

Note

After deleting cookies, return to the Center for Democracy & Technology site (http://opt-out.cdt.org/featured) and opt out again.

You can also manually delete cookies. If you use Internet Explorer, navigate to c:\Windows\Temporary Internet Files and C:\Windows\Cookies and delete all the contents of both folders. If you use Netscape, search for a file named cookies.txt and delete it.

Web Bugs

Web bugs are invisible graphics files that load with a Web page. They're so tiny you can't see the little buggers! Web bugs reveal to the server that initiated the bug your computer's unique IP address and the location of the page you're browsing. From then on, that Web bug can identify you by your cookie settings, track you, and profile you. Because Web bugs are basically minute graphics files, you won't be bugged if you disable image loading in your browser—but you won't see any graphics, either! That's a tradeoff most computer users won't make.

The best ways to defeat Web bugs is to follow these steps.

1. Block cookies.
2. Delete cookies.
3. Use Ad-aware and SpyBot Search & Destroy to scan for spyware regularly.

Clear Your Web Browser's Cache Memory

Every time you surf the Web, copies of the pages you visit (including images, cookies, and Web bugs) are saved in your computer's browser cache. This makes Web browsing faster, but it has the disadvantage of leaving on your hard drive a trail of where you've been. This can be particularly troublesome for those who share a computer. In fact, these files leave every computer system more vulnerable to hacking!

To clear the cache memory in Internet Explorer 6

1. Click Tools on Internet Explorer's menu bar.
2. Click Internet Options.
3. Click the Delete Files button under Temporary Internet Files.

Clear Your Web Browser's History

Many a boss has spied on his secretary by examining her Web browser's history. Most people are unaware that Internet Explorer is capable of remembering every Web page they have ever visited. In IE 6, the default can be set to a maximum of 999 days!

To clear the browser history in Internet Explorer 6

1. Click Tools on Internet Explorer's menu bar.
2. Click Internet Options.
3. Click the Clear History button under History.

Disable AutoComplete

Internet Explorer has a convenient feature that remembers all your user names, passwords, and personal information (such as your name, address, phone number, and e-mail address). Unfortunately, this feature is prone to being hacked.

To disable AutoComplete in Internet Explorer 6

1. Click Tools on Internet Explorer's menu bar.
2. Click Internet Options.
3. Click the Content tab.
4. Click the AutoComplete button
5. Uncheck (or check) the AutoComplete functions you want to disable or use, respectively.
6. Click the Clear Forms and Clear Passwords buttons.

Secure Sockets Layer

SSL (*Secure Sockets Layer*) is a secure protocol for transmitting private information over the Internet. SSL works by using a public key to encrypt the data being transferred. Web sites use SSL to securely obtain confidential information, such as credit card numbers, from users. The only circumstance under which you can safely provide confidential information over the Internet is with an SSL connection!

There are two ways to tell whether a connection is an SSL connection.

> **Https://**. If the URL has an "S" after "HTTP," as in HTTPS://, it's an SSL connection.

> **Safety lock icon**. If a safety lock icon appears in the lower-right corner of your Web browser's status bar (Figure 13.6), the connection is an SSL connection.

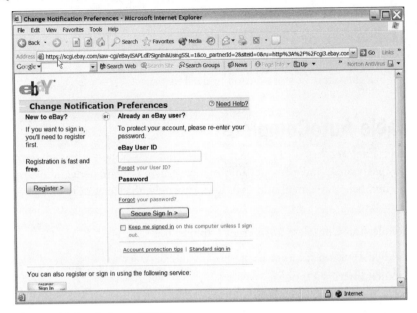

Figure 13.6 *An https:// URL*

The First Step to Protect Yourself on the Internet

Never provide confidential information over the Web to a URL that doesn't begin with https://, and always look for the safety lock icon on your Web browser's status bar!

E-Mail and Its Evil Twin

E-mail was the Internet's first Killer app, but spam, its evil twin, is the bane of the Internet. Avoiding spam is an art, but there's more to e-mail than dodging spam. Even the most innocuous messages can hide Trojan horses and viruses. E-mail is notoriously insecure!

Following are some tips for avoiding e-mail's downside.

➤ Delete all unsolicited e-mail without opening it.

➤ Don't reveal your e-mail address unless it's absolutely necessary.

- Create separate e-mail accounts for different functions (such as e-commerce, business, technical support, family, friends, and user groups).
- Create a separate e-mail inbox for spam.
- Encrypt sensitive e-mail.
- Don't allow your e-mail address to be included in any online membership directories. (If it's already listed, insist that it be removed!)
- Never provide credit card or personal information in an e-mail.
- Never open file attachments from a merchant or stranger.
- Never open messages with pictures from a merchant or stranger.
- Never click on hyperlinks from a merchant or stranger.
- Use a spam filter.
- Use a spam blocker.

Spam Blockers

Many people use spam blockers. I don't, so I can't recommend one. In my experience spam blockers are conflict-prone, they hog system resources and slow down mail delivery, and they aren't bulletproof. Spam still gets through and occasionally legitimate messages don't! Then there's the question of spyware, which I consider a greater scourge than spam. If a shareware spam blocker installs adware or spyware on your system, as many do, the solution is worse than the problem!

Anti-Spam Plan

Short of anti-spam legislation, which will effectively outlaw it, there is no simple solution to spam. Ironically, the Eighth Circuit Court of Appeals' recent ruling against fax.com (which essentially stated that unsolicited fax advertisements are not protected by the First Amendment's guarantee of freedom of expression) sets a new precedent that should hasten laws that restrict unsolicited e-mail.

Spammers Can't Spam What They Can't Find

I hate to keep repeating myself, but stealth is the most effective way to dodge spam. Spammers can't spam what they can't find! Unfortunately, this solution is not foolproof. Spammers are capable of bulk e-mailing every user at a given portal using name-randomizing technology that spits out almost every possible alpha-numeric combination. That proviso aside, not giving out your e-mail address is the best way to avoid getting spam.

Delete All Unsolicited E-Mail without Opening It

This is a no-brainer. The only way to deal with spam is to never open it! Delete spam unopened. Never respond to it! When you open spam formatted in HTML, the e-mail can communicate with the spammer's server, indicating that you're a live one! To be safe, delete all unsolicited e-mail in your inbox without opening it. If you use Outlook, Outlook Express, or Netscape, turn off the preview pane so you don't unwittingly pull HTML code from some spammer.

To deactivate the preview pane in Outlook

1. Navigate to your inbox in Outlook.
2. Click the View menu.
3. Uncheck the Preview Pane option.

Spam Filters

A spam filter is not a spam blocker, which is software that piggybacks on your e-mail program. A spam filter is built into your e-mail program. When you receive spam, you can add the sender to a Junk Senders list, which automatically deletes messages from that sender in the future. Refer to your particular e-mail program for instructions. I've provided the steps for adding senders to the Junk Senders list in Outlook.

To add senders to the junk e-mail list in Outlook

> Right click on a spam message.
> Click Junk E-Mail.
> Click Add to Junk Senders List.

To automatically and permanently delete spam in Outlook:

1. Click Rules Wizard on Outlook's Tools menu.
2. Click New.
3. Check Start from a Blank Rule.
4. Select Check Messages When They Arrive.

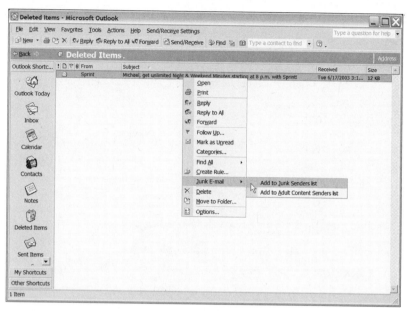

Figure 13.7 *Outlook's Junk Senders list*

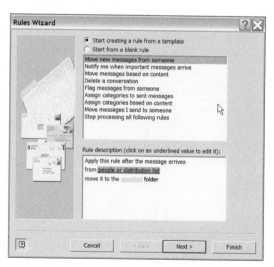

Figure 13.8 *The Outlook Rules Wizard*

5. Click Next.

6. Check Suspected to Be Junk E-Mail from Junk Senders.

7. Check Permanently Delete It.

8. Click OK when you receive a message about not being able to recover the spam.

9. Click Finish.

You can also screen spam by deleting e-mail messages that contain keywords like "Viagra," "loan," "credit," "porn," "rich," "hot," "DVD," and "weight" in the Subject line. I've added more than 60 such words to my Outlook filter list.

To delete spam by filtering keywords in Outlook:

1. Click Rules Wizard on Outlook's Tools menu.

2. Click New.

3. Check Start Creating a Rule from a Template.

4. Select Move Messages Based on Content.

5. click "Apply this rule after the message arrives with <u>specific words (underlined).</u>"

6. In the Search Text box specify the word you want to filter such as "loan."

7. Click Add, then OK

8. In the Rules Description box specify the Deleted Items folder as the <u>specified folder</u> (<u>underlined</u>) to move the messages to.

9. Click Next three times.

10. Specify a nane for the Rule.

11. Click Finish.

Instant Messaging

If you use a consumer IM program from AOL, MSN, or Yahoo!, beware! Two buffer-overflow vulnerabilities were recently discovered in AOL Instant Messenger. These vulnerabilities would have allowed attackers to run code on your computer and control it remotely. AOL claims they fixed the problem on their servers, but you should upgrade to the latest version of AIM just to play it safe.

In older versions of MSN Messenger and MSN Chat Control, an ActiveX control that lets you create online chat rooms has a vulnerability that could allow an attacker to run code on your computer. Microsoft has a patch for it (Security Bulletin MS02-022), but you should upgrade to the latest version of MSN Messenger to be safe. Older versions of Yahoo! Messenger also contain security flaws that allow hackers to run code on your computer, so you should also upgrade to the latest version of Yahoo! Messenger.

Consumer instant-messaging programs don't use encryption, which means your information is subject to hacking. IM also advertises your whereabouts. It's a prime example of presence awareness technology, described in Chapter 6. If you use an instant-messaging program, keep security in the front of your mind. If you don't use IM, and MSN's annoying MSN Messenger icon pops up every time you boot, know that Microsoft designed it that way and you have to disable it! If you have Outlook, you might even have to disable it twice.

To disable MSN Instant Messenger from loading (in Internet Explorer 6)

1. Click the Tools menu in Internet Explorer 6.
2. Uncheck Windows Messenger (if it's checked).

To disable MSN Instant Messenger from loading (in Outlook)

1. Click Options on Outlook's Tools menu.
2. Click the Other tab.
3. Uncheck Enable Instant Messaging in MS Outlook (if it's checked).

Downloads and Spyware

Eminem's latest album, naughty pictures of Pamela Anderson and Tommy Lee, free software...downloads are the Internet's second killer app! They're also the Internet's primary source of spyware, viruses, and Trojan horses. If you're broke and you can't afford the price tag of clean shareware, find an ad-free, non-spyware equivalent of the program you need. Avoid spyware at all costs! Before you download and install shareware, surf over to http://www.spychecker.com or http://www.spywareinfo.com and check whether the program is listed in their spyware database. Also, do a virus check on all files that you download from the Internet prior to installation.

Figure 13.9 *The Spywareinfo Web site*

Online Scams

The number of complaints referred to law enforcement authorities by the FBI's Internet Fraud Complaint Center (IFCC) went from 16,775 in 2001 to 48,252 in 2002. In that timeframe, the amount of money lost more than tripled, from $17 million to $54 million. In 2002, identity theft on the Internet increased by a whopping 73 percent! Following are a few intriguing statistics.

- Victims of identity theft lost an average of $2,000 each.
- Online-auction fraud accounted for 46 percent of all complaints.
- The median per-person loss for the Nigerian letter scam was the highest, at $3,864.
- The median per-person loss for check fraud was $1,100.
- The majority of dot-com victims live in California, New York, Florida, Texas, and Illinois.

Web Spoofing

Web spoofing is a new kind of digital con game in which attackers create a convincing but false copy of a Web site you know and trust. The spoofed site looks just like the real one; it has the same pages, graphics, and links. However, the attacker controls the site, so that all traffic between the victim's browser and the Web goes through the spoofer's computer. A spoofing attack sets up the victim to do something that would be entirely appropriate if the false world were real, such as entering his or her user name and password.

eBay and a cross-section of its 55 million users were targets of a convincing Web spoof in December 2002. The perpetrators reportedly set up a fake eBay that mimicked the auction site right down to its artwork, color scheme, and logos. The scammers somehow acquired a number of eBay users' e-mail addresses, and then sent an authentic-looking message requesting that the recipients log on to a secure hyperlink (www.ebayupdates.com) and re-enter financial data such as their credit card numbers and bank account numbers.

```
----Original Message----
From: eBay Billing
Sent: Thursday, Dec. 3, 2002 11:23 PM
To: eBayUserX@ISP.com
Subject: Billing Error

Dear eBay Member,

We at eBay are sorry to inform you that we are having problems with
the billing information of your account. Please use the following
link to log on to eBay and update your account information.
```

eBay quickly got wind of the scheme and had the fake auction site shut down. But by that point, countless users had been stung and the damage was already done. Unfortunately, some people are more gullible than others are!

This was not the first instance of identity theft perpetrated on a spoof eBay site. It must be noted, however, that eBay bears no responsibility for this kind of hoax. The best it can do is sound a clarion call that scams are part of the auction game and instruct its members on how to avoid them. eBay has always gone the extra mile in that regard.

Auction fraud accounts for 46 percent of all online complaints. Following is a recap that I found on the Security Center of PayPal (http://www.paypal.com/cgi-bin/webscr?cmd=p/gen/security-main-outside), which is now owned by eBay. Investing an hour of your time to learn the ground rules before you conduct business on the Internet could save you a lot of grief! The same rules that apply to online auctions generally conform to all Internet commerce.

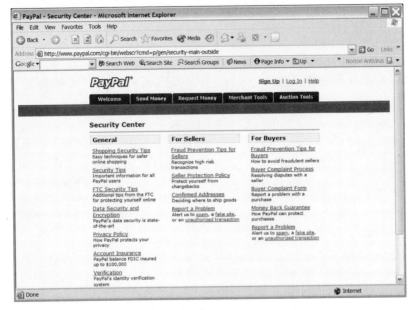

Figure 13.10 *The PayPal Security Center*

Online auction security tips:

> ➤ Know your seller. (Check the seller's feedback.)
> ➤ Compare listings. (Be suspicious of hard-to-find items offered at low prices.)
> ➤ Don't sacrifice caution for an impulse buy.
> ➤ Use extra caution with high-demand items.
> ➤ Ask before you buy.
> ➤ Be wary of items with delayed shipment.
> ➤ Do not buy items "out of auction" (the Jason Eric Smith rule).
> ➤ If it sounds too good to be true, it probably is.
> ➤ Never share your password with anyone.
> ➤ Don't use the same password for other online services, such as AOL, MSN, or Yahoo!
> ➤ Never access a Web site by clicking on an e-mail hyperlink.
> ➤ Use a secure SSL connection.

Online auction warning signs:

> ➤ Seller has large quantities of hard-to-find items.
> ➤ Seller buys low-dollar items to improve his or her feedback rating, and then lists high-ticket items to rip off bidders.

➤ Seller lists multiple items with the same picture.

➤ The expected delivery date is more than 20 days after payment.

Fraud prevention tips for sellers:

➤ Ship to the buyer's confirmed address.

➤ Use a shipping service with online tracking.

➤ Check out the buyer's feedback rating and reputation.

➤ Accept payment from only one PayPal account per buyer.

➤ Limit credit card payments.

➤ Be wary of buyers who are not concerned with costs.

➤ Conduct more research on buyers of high-value items.

➤ Be extra cautious with non-U.S. payments.

I'm obviously a big fan of online auctions (and eBay in particular), which is why I wrote *Confessions of an Internet Auction Junkie* a few years ago. But even if 99 percent of eBay's transactions go through without a hitch, as the company claims, that still leaves hundreds of thousands of complaints each year, a majority of which involve fraud. It's incumbent on eBay to make its site as secure as possible. Unfortunately, I occasionally encounter security holes and lapses on eBay's part.

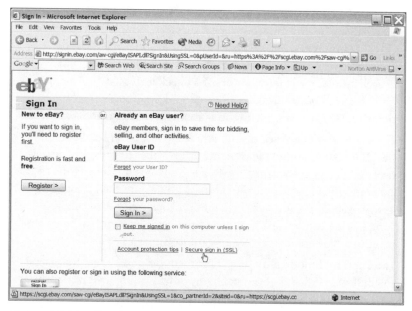

Figure 13.11 *eBay non-secure seller sign-in*

For the life of me, I don't understand how in this day and age eBay can have a non-secure log-on page by default. But it does! When you click Sell on eBay, you're directed to a non-SSL sign-in page where you're prompted to enter your user name and password. Directly below, eBay provides a link to a secure sign-in page. So why not provide SSL sign-in by default? I find security lapses like this all over the Internet. No site, large or small, is above security blunders.

Dot-Cons

Con artists have gone high-tech! Whether they're using the excitement of an Internet auction, applying new technology to peddle traditional business scams, using e-mail to reach vast numbers of people with false promises, or hijacking consumers' modems and cramming hefty long-distance charges onto their phone bills, scam artists are just a click away. Fortunately, law enforcement is on the case. Using complaints to Consumer Sentinel, a fraud database, as their guide, the FTC has identified the top-ten dot-cons facing consumers on the Web. The following information was gleaned from the Web site of the FTC at http://www.ftc.gov/bcp/conline/edcams/dotcon/.

1. **Internet auctions**. After sending their money, consumers receive an item that is less valuable than promised—or worse, they don't receive anything at all.

2. **Long-distance and Internet access services**. Simply by cashing a check, consumers have been trapped into long-term contracts for Internet access or long-distance services with big penalties for cancellation or early termination. If a check arrives at your home or business, read both sides carefully and look inside the envelope to find the conditions you're agreeing to if you cash the check.

3. **Porn site credit card scam**. The lure is to view adult images online for free, but you must provide a credit card number to prove the user is over 18. The porn site then runs up big charges on the victim's credit card, and the victim is too embarrassed to dispute them. You should always dispute unauthorized charges on your credit card bill by complaining to the bank that issued the card. Federal law limits your liability to $50 in charges if your card is misused.

4. **International modem dialing**. This scam promises users free access to adult material and pornography by downloading a viewer or dialer program. The dialing program then disconnects the modem and reconnects to the Internet using an international long-distance

number. Victims are then billed exorbitant long-distance charges on their phone bills.

5. **Web cramming.** Charges for a supposedly free custom-designed Web site or other service are billed to the victim's phone bill.

6. **Multilevel marketing plans (pyramids).** The idea of a making money through products you sell, as well as those sold by people you recruit into the program, backfires when the products don't sell and people decline to be recruited. Avoid plans that require you to recruit distributors, buy expensive inventory, or commit to a minimum sales volume.

7. **Travel and vacation.** The promise of a luxurious trip with lots of extras at a bargain-basement price is destroyed when the tourist receives lousy accommodations or no trip at all. Get references for any travel company with whom you plan to do business. Then get details of the trip in writing, including the cancellation policy, before you sign up for anything.

8. **Business opportunities.** Taken in by promises of excellent earnings, many consumers have invested in biz ops that turned out to be biz flops! Talk to other people who started businesses through the same company, get all the promises in writing, and study the proposed contract carefully before signing.

9. **Investments.** In this scam, the promise of huge returns after investment in a day-trading system or a service that claims to be able to predict the market with 100 percent accuracy backfires and the victim loses money. Be wary of extravagant claims about performance or earning potential.

10. **Healthcare products.** The promise that items not sold through traditional suppliers are proven to cure serious and even fatal health problems can delay seriously ill people from getting the health care they need. Consult a healthcare professional before buying any cure-all that claims to treat a wide range of ailments or offers quick cures and easy solutions to serious illnesses.

CHAPTER 14
The Public Zone

- ➣ Don't Fit the Profile
- ➣ Develop a Public Persona
- ➣ Identity Theft
- ➣ Credit Card Skimming
- ➣ Workplace Privacy

When I think of the Public Zone, two things immediately spring to mind—surveillance and the looming potential for catastrophe. I'm not just talking about the threat of terrorism. A couple of recent public catastrophes were the fire at The Station nightclub in Rhode Island that killed 96 people and injured hundreds more, and the stampede at the E2 disco in Chicago that crushed 21 club-goers to death the same week; neither of these was caused by terrorism. This leads me to the first rule of avoiding public catastrophe.

Devise a Vigilant Exit Strategy

Whenever you're in public, and this includes the common areas of your own apartment building, devise a vigilant exit strategy for common worst-case scenarios—fires, earthquakes, floods, explosions, and random acts of violence. The first thing to do when you're at your workplace, the movies, a mall, a stadium, a nightclub, a restaurant, an airport, or when you board an airplane is to check the location of the exits and figure out how to reach them in case of an emergency!

The Best Way to Avoid Danger

Use your common sense! If it looks dangerous, it probably is. Avoid dark streets, bad neighborhoods, seedy crowds, and crowded places!

Don't Fit the Profile

I would just like to say that it is my conviction that longer hair and other flamboyant affectations of appearance are nothing more than the male's emergence from his drab camouflage into the gaudy plumage which is the birthright of his sex.

—*Hair*

The above was true when the hit musical *Hair* ran on Broadway. I know because I was a hippie! But in this era of elevated security alerts, it's unwise to draw attention to your appearance or behavior. I wish I could say that you should do your own thing, but if you look like a gang-banger, biker, skinhead, pimp, shoplifter, junkie, or whatever the current profile of a terrorist is, you will get hassled!

Computer profiling is standard operating procedure since 9/11, backed by the full authority of federal, state, and local law enforcement, by provisions under the USA Patriot Act, the Homeland Security Act, and the Total Information Awareness (TIA) program (renamed the Terrorism Information Awareness program by the Bush Administration after embarrassment over the spy-like sound of the original name).

Bush was also forced to fire the TIA's controversial creator, Admiral John Poindexter, who was also fired as the Reagan Administration's National Security Advisor after being convicted of conspiracy, lying to Congress, defrauding the government, and destroying evidence in the Iran-Contra scandal. Just the kind of guy you want to have as our country's super-snoop!

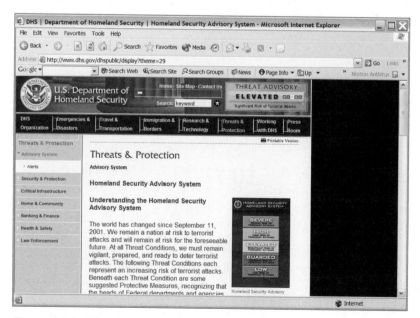

Figure 14.1 *Homeland Security Advisory System Web site*

Develop a Public Persona

Even if you have a proclivity for dressing like one of the Village People in private, it's prudent to develop a public persona that doesn't fit the profile. Be aware of your surroundings at all times, and look like you know where you're going—even if you don't! Muggers typically look for people with lost looks on their faces.

An American flag T-shirt is fine to wear to a Fourth of July picnic, but that same T-shirt could backfire if you wear it to a Bastille Day parade in France! In other words, dress for the occasion.

Security Checkpoints

It doesn't matter where you are—cruising on Sunset Boulevard or at a rock concert, a sporting event, a nightclub, or an airport—sooner or later you'll encounter a security checkpoint. Present your ID and be cooperative. Answer all reasonable questions. When it comes to being searched, remember that entertainment and travel are optional choices; you elected to be there. Random searches are a reality in the Public Zone!

Air Travel

When you fly, your body and luggage are subject to search. That's the law! In March 2003, the Transportation Security Administration (TSA) started testing a second-generation airline passenger profiling system known as the Computer Assisted Passenger Pre-Screening System II (CAPPS-II). The system is being developed in collaboration with Lockheed Martin Management & Data Systems. According to a description on the TSA Web site, the system can confirm a passenger's identity and any potential security threat they might pose in less than five seconds.

Under a proposed plan, the TSA will require every US commercial air carrier to supply them with passenger information collected during the reservation and ticketing process. That information will then be combined with financial and personal data contained in government and commercial databases to determine a risk score for every passenger.

> ➤ **Low risk**. This will require cursory personal and luggage screening.
> ➤ **High risk**. This will require a full body and luggage search.
> ➤ **Flight ban**. This will include suspected terrorists on a federal watch list who are banned from US air travel.

This plan is evoking a maelstrom of protest from civil rights organizations, which question the efficacy of such profiling and denounce it as an invasion of privacy and civil liberties.

Keep Your ID Handy

Unfortunately, we have come to a point in time when presenting your ID at public checkpoints is mandatory. Be prepared to present it. I hate to put it this way, but…have your papers in order!

Protect Your Wallet and Purse from Theft

Keep your ID in your wallet or purse and protect it from theft! If you lose your wallet, you're screwed. If it gets stolen, you're plumb out of luck! Cash, ID, credit cards, driver's license, health insurance card with your Social Security Number on it, your signature—when you get your pocket picked, you're going to get your identity stolen!

If you want to know how to protect a wallet or purse, ask a pickpocket. That's exactly what I did! I asked Gene Turner, the renowned pickpocket and night-club entertainer. Here are some of Turner's tips and tricks.

➤ Be aware of your surroundings, especially in crowded places. Be aware of bumps, commotions, and aggressive people.

➤ Beware of signs that tell you to beware of pickpockets. They could be a ploy by pickpockets to help spot your valuables. Men check their wallets and the women check their jewelry. People invariably check their most expensive items first.

➤ Don't flash cash or wear valuables in public. Don't wear expensive jewelry if you are going to be in a crowd or an unfamiliar place.

➤ Wear a money belt. Don't carry large sums of cash. If you must carry a lot of money, always keep it in a money belt under your clothing. Spread pocket money among several pockets. Pickpockets can only pick one pocket at a time.

➤ Don't carry valuables in a backpack or fanny pack. Anyone can reach into a backpack without you seeing or feeling it. If you use a fanny pack, you should wear it in the front and, if possible, make sure the buckle is in the front so a pickpocket will have a more difficult time releasing the latch without your knowledge.

➤ Don't let anyone else carry your luggage. That's the best way to lose it!

Figure 14.2 *Gene Turner's photo on pickpocket.com*

Wallet tips:

- ➤ Don't carry your wallet in your back pocket. Men feel that if the pocket is buttoned the wallet is safe, but a good pickpocket can lift a wallet every time. Some pickpockets even use a razorblade to slit the bottom of the pocket so the wallet drops into their waiting hands!

- ➤ Put your wallet in your pocket sideways. Also place wide rubber bands around your wallet. It will be more difficult for a pickpocket to get the wallet out of your pocket—more difficult, but not impossible!

- ➤ Know where your credit card is at all times. After you use it, put it back in your wallet or purse. Don't place it in your pocket!

Purse tips:

- ➤ Use handbags and purses that have zippers or lock latches.

- ➤ Always keep your handbag or purse zipped or latched.

- ➤ Carry your handbag in front of you.

- ➤ If your handbag or purse has a flap to open, keep the flap against your body.

Identity Theft

The stripe on a credit or ATM card is magnetized. The data is analog, not digital; therefore, it is easy to decipher. A card reader is not unlike the head on a tape deck; it reads the information like recorded music. The stripe on the back of bank cards has three tracks of data that contain information such as account number, accountholder's name, card expiration date, and PIN code. There is also a field for discretionary data, which might include further security information or links to other accounts.

Credit Card Skimming

How would society function without the ubiquitous magnetic card reader? Card readers are found virtually everywhere that business is conducted. But there's a dark side: Skimmers, or *wedges*, as they're sometimes known, are small battery-powered card readers used by criminals to steal credit card data from unsuspecting customers. In most rings, skimming is performed by waiters, salespeople, clerks, or anyone involved with handling a credit card. The waiter takes your card, leaves the table, reaches under his apron, and presto, swipes your card through the skimmer in less than a second! In some cases criminals don't even bother to conceal the skimmer from the victim. They wear it audaciously on their belt, and the victim has no inkling what they are looking at.

In a recent raid in Queens, New York, detectives discovered a laptop computer containing 4,300 stolen card numbers that had been skimmed from patrons throughout New York, New Jersey, and Connecticut. The ring had equipment to make counterfeit cards, including legitimate blank cards probably stolen from American Express and MasterCard. Credit card skimming is on the rise. When you're out in public, keep one eye on your credit card and the other one on the lookout for skimmers!

Figure 14.3 *A credit card skimmer*

Dispose of Credit Card Receipts Properly

Identity thieves can do almost as much with carelessly discarded credit card receipts as they can with the credit card itself. Your name, credit card number, and signature are on that innocuous little slip of paper. Don't leave it behind on some restaurant table or litter the public sidewalk with it. Take credit card receipts with you and dispose of them securely.

Workplace Surveillance

Big Brother is watching! At a casino in Atlantic City, an infrared sensor keeps a computer log that tracks each time an employee fails to wash his or her hands after using the bathroom. At a college in Massachusetts, a secretary was informed that a camera installed to deter nighttime intruders had instead captured her changing clothes in the privacy of her own office during the day. An employee at a company that produces porn was fired because he spent too much time on eBay and not enough time watching porn. These are but a few examples of workplace surveillance cited by Frederick Lane in his new book, *The Naked Employee: How Technology is Compromising Workplace Privacy* (AMACOM, 2003). As Lane describes in Chapter 6, 14 million employees—more than one-third of the American workforce—have their Internet or e-mail under continuous workplace surveillance. In most cases it's legal, but the least you can do is ascertain whether you're being watched. Be discrete and sniff around.

How might your employer be spying on you? There are several ways.

> **Telephone.** The ACLU estimates that employers eavesdrop on about 400 million telephone calls annually. Federal wiretap laws forbid eavesdropping on conversations unless one of the parties in the conversation consents, but the Electronic Communications Privacy Act of 1986 allows employers to listen to job-related conversations. A recent American Management Association (AMA) study estimates that 12 percent of employees' phone calls and 8 percent of their voicemail is reviewed in the workplace.

> **Closed-circuit television.** The same AMA study estimates that 15 percent of the American workforce is monitored by closed-circuit TV (CCTV).

- ➤ **Packet sniffers**. A packet sniffer is a program that can monitor information you send over your company's network. With a packet sniffer, your system administrator can ascertain who you send e-mail to, the content of the text, the Web sites you visit, and what you download.

- ➤ **Desktop-monitoring programs**. Every keystroke you type sends a signal from the keyboard to an application. Desktop-monitoring programs, such as iSpyNOW, monitor every keystroke by intercepting the signal and recording it stroke-for-stroke. System administrators usually install the monitoring software, but keystroke interceptors are also a popular way for hackers to steal passwords.

- ➤ **Log files**. Your computer is full of log files that provide evidence of what you've done. With these log files, a system administrator can determine what Web sites you've accessed, to and from whom you're sending and receiving e-mail, and what applications you've been using.

Workplace Privacy

Forget about it! American courts tend to favor the employer in workplace-surveillance cases. The US Constitution contains no express right to privacy, but the US Supreme Court has historically upheld an implied right to privacy. This right doesn't apply to employees, however. The courts seem to uphold the idea that because the company owns the equipment and office space, it has a right to monitor its employees to prevent misuse of that equipment and space. For this reason, you should always be prudent when logging onto the Internet and sending e-mail. Choose your words carefully. You never know who might be reading them!

Photo Enforcement

The consensus of opinion is photo enforcement is an effective deterrent to traffic accidents triggered by drivers who run red lights. I make a conscious effort to detour around photo enforcement, however. People drive unpredictably around photo-enforced traffic lights; they either speed up or slow down. In my empirical observation photo enforcement alters logical behavior and impedes the normal flow of traffic. That's why I avoid photo enforcement like the plague!

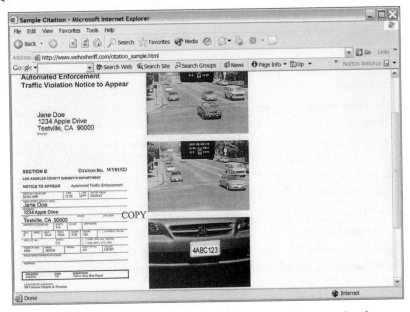

Figure 14.4 *West Hollywood Sheriff's Station photo enforcement site photos*

I actually have nightmares about receiving a $271 ticket from my city in the mail. And I don't run red lights! Photo-enforcement citations amount to nothing less than a stealth tax. The top three causes of traffic accidents are inattention, failure to yield, and DUI. Photo-enforcement cameras do nothing to prevent these kinds of accidents. Experts believe that improved roadway engineering, lengthening of the yellow-light phase, and better signage are the best ways to prevent traffic accidents. In my opinion photo enforcement is just another example of how Kafkaesque society has become.

That's All, Folks!

By now you know I have very strong opinions when it comes to the subject of privacy. My objective in writing this book was not to sway your opinion but to provide you with enough facts and information to draw your own. I could go on but feel I've met my objective. I hope this book helps you in you everyday life and that you enjoyed reading it. Good luck!

Index

X–Z